Create Your Own

Digital Movies

PAM STRAYER

SAMS   800 East 96th Street, Indianapolis, Indiana 46240 USA

Create Your Own Digital Movies

Copyright © 2006 by Sams Publishing

International Standard Book Number: 0-672-32834-8

Library of Congress Catalog Card Number: 2005930223

Printed in the United States of America

First Printing: October 2005

08 07 06 05   4 3 2 1

Trademarks

All terms mentioned in this book that are known to be trademarks or service marks have been appropriately capitalized. Sams Publishing cannot attest to the accuracy of this information. Use of a term in this book should not be regarded as affecting the validity of any trademark or service mark.

Warning and Disclaimer

Bulk Sales

Sams Publishing offers excellent discounts on this book when ordered in quantity for bulk purchases or special sales. For more information, please contact

U.S. Corporate and Government Sales
1-800-382-3419
corpsales@pearsontechgroup.com

For sales outside of the U.S., please contact

International Sales
international@pearsoned.com

Publisher
Paul Boger

Acquisitions Editor
Loretta Yates

Development Editor
Mark Renfrow

Managing Editor
Charlotte Clapp

Senior Project Editor
Matthew Purcell

Copy Editor
Kitty Jarrett

Indexer
Aaron Black

Proofreader
Paula Lowell

Technical Editor
Kate Binder

Publishing Coordinator
Cindy Teeters

Multimedia Developer
Dan Scherf

Designer
Gary Adair

Page Layout
Julie Parks
Jeff Henn

Contents at a Glance

Table of Contents

About the Author

Pam Strayer has been a documentary filmmaker since the mid-1980s and a writer/producer involved in creative projects on the digital frontier since 1992 when she was part of the creative team that made the million-selling CD-ROM *From Alice to Ocean*, a landmark Quicktime 1.0 project that marked the debut of video on computers. She has written numerous books for Apple and taught and lectured on multimedia widely from San Francisco to Provence. The recipient of fellowships from PBS, the American Film Institute, and London-based Artec, she has also created interactive television projects (for Time Warner) and large-scale, dynamic websites. Her client list includes PBS, CPB, Time Warner, Apple, IBM, Intel, Healthcentral.com, DNA.com, HandHeld entertainment, Jerry Garcia, UN Secretary Boutros Boutros Ghali, and the Dalai Lama. For more information and online links to resources in this book, visit her website at www.createyourowndigitalmovies.com.

Dedication

I dedicate this book to Bill Jersey.

We Want to Hear from You!

As the reader of this book, *you* are our most important critic and commentator. We value your opinion and want to know what we're doing right, what we could do better, what areas you would like to see us publish in, and any other words of wisdom you're willing to pass our way.

Please note that I cannot help you with technical problems related to the topic of this book. We do have a User Services group, however, where I will forward specific technical questions related to the book.

When you write, please be sure to include this book's title and author as well as your name, email address, and phone number. I will carefully review your comments and share them with the author and editors who worked on the book.

Email: feedback@samspublishing.com

Mail: Paul Boger
          Publisher
          Sams Publishing
          800 East 96th Street
          Indianapolis, IN 46240 USA

For more information about this book or another Sams Publishing title, visit our website at www.samspublishing.com. Type the ISBN (excluding hyphens) or the title of a book in the Search field to find the page you're looking for.

INTRODUCTION

Welcome to *Create Your Own Digital Movies*

Congratulations on getting started learning how to make movies using your personal computer. You'll find that it's easy and fun to shoot, edit, and share videos with your family members and friends . Did you know that you don't have to learn *every* feature in your editing software, and you don't have to learn the entire software program to get started? In this book, you'll learn a few basics first and then enjoy a project-oriented approach to help you get started and succeed in making great movies.

Making great movies is 75% about shooting well and 25% about editing well. If you learn how to shoot lively, interesting footage, your movies will shine. Whereas most video how-to books concentrate on editing alone, this book helps you develop *all* the skills—including both shooting and editing—you need to make great videos!

First, you'll learn how to make movies for any occasion, and then you'll move on to specific, in-depth chapters that guide you step-by-step in making some of the most popular kinds of movies. In the first four chapters, you'll get these essentials:

- ▶ **An overview on equipment basics**—You'll learn about what you need in the way of a camcorder, accessories, a PC, and editing software.
- ▶ **How to shoot**—You'll learn the basic building blocks for making movies.

▸ **How to edit**—You'll learn the specific skills you need to use Movie Maker, along with general advice on how to edit well.

▸ **How to share your movies**—You'll learn how to share your movies on the Web, via DVD, and more.

In addition, you'll learn the specifics of shooting and editing great-looking movies for specific situations, as discussed in the following chapters:

▸ Chapter 5, "Project 1: Creating Birthday Party and Baby Movies"

▸ Chapter 6, "Project 2: Making Travel or Vacation Movies"

▸ Chapter 7, "Project 3: Making Sporting Event Movies"

▸ Chapter 8, "Project 4: Making School Play (and Other Live Event) Movies"

▸ Chapter 9, "Project 5: Making Family Memory Movies"

Are you interested in making great video, and do you want to learn *only what you need to know* to shoot and edit your first movies? Then this book is for you!

This book teaches you only what you need to know to get started making movies. When you understand the basic skills, you'll be able to make movies for many different kinds of occasions:

▸ **Baby and birthday party movies**—By making birthday party and baby movies, you can share happy moments in life with your family and friends.

▸ **Vacation and travel movies**—You can make the memories of a trip last long after the suitcase is unpacked by recording your adventures and sharing them with others.

▸ **Sports movies**—You can capture all the action of your favorite sports team or family athlete by making sports movies.

▸ **School and other live-event movies**—You can video all the fun of music and other performances and share your movies with your family or the whole class.

▸ **Family memory movies**—You can edit together photos, audio, old films, and VHS movies, as well as new video footage that you shoot to preserve precious family memories.

Are you using software other than Movie Maker? Or editing on a Mac? Although this book provides specific information on Movie Maker software for the PC, it provides plenty of help in making great movies, no matter what editing software or computer you use.

With a wealth of information on video equipment, shooting and shot lists, general editing skills and techniques, and essential information on how to share movies, this book will teach you—quickly and easily—how to create your own digital movies from start to finish, and you'll learn only what you need to know.

So get started and enjoy the excitement of creating your first movies!

CHAPTER 1

Welcome to the Wonderful World of Digital Video

To see just how easy it is to make your own movies, check out *New York Times* technology columnist David Pogue's online movies, which are available from the *New York Times* website. You can find the movie, dated March 2, 2005, by using the Multimedia Search on the www.nytimes.com advanced search page, selecting the video check box, and typing One-Man Studio. Or go straight to www.nytimes.com/video/html/2005/03/02/technology/20050303_pogue_VIDEO.html.

Every week Pogue creates an informal, funny movie about the latest developments in technology (see Figure 1.1). (I highly recommend them, for the information as well as the entertainment value he brings to each 2- to 4-minute program.)

FIGURE 1.1
David Pogue's "A One-Man Studio."

In "A One-Man Studio," Pogue explains how he received a letter from a major technology company executive, asking him about his production staff for shooting these weekly movies. The letter made him laugh out loud. His "production staff" is just one person: him.

He scripts, shoots, and edits his movies himself. That's right. He even shoots himself on camera,

In this book, you'll discover how easy it is to create your videos, starting with understanding what you need for a basic desktop video system: a camcorder and a personal computer with movie editing software.

Many of us have tried digital photography and enjoyed taking pictures cheaply and sharing them on the Internet. The same is becoming true with movies: You can shoot and edit video and share it with anyone and everyone.

Video gives us a great opportunity to capture life as it happens and share it with others. The cameras, your computer, the software…today all these tools make it easy. Or at least that's what I hope you'll learn from this book. It gets even easier when you understand that making different kinds of video projects is based on predictable, orderly steps and a variety of techniques. Making each kind of video has a certain number of steps in the process—all of which are organized for you in the chapters in this book.

When you master the basic skills—which requires an initial investment of time and energy—you'll find that making and sharing your movies *will* get easier and can become a compelling hobby. Making your first movie is an exercise in faith and in building confidence; you *can* do it (*children* are doing it!). This book shows you how to master just enough of the skills you need to make your own movies, without having to know every single feature of your camcorder or editing software.

After you've shot and edited your first video, you may be surprised at how easy and enjoyable making movies is. After you've made the initial equipment investment, creating movies is very inexpensive. Beware, though: You could get hooked!

The big picture of what's happening today is that anyone can make his or her own movies—including you.

Great Shooting = Easy Editing

Over the years, I've taught some of my friends how to make movies and learned from watching their mistakes and successes. It takes a little while for people to understand how to edit movies, but soon the attention turns to what they shot. As the expression goes: garbage in, garbage out.

Although it's important to learn how to edit, the best advice anyone can give you is to learn how to shoot. This book helps you by providing in-depth shooting suggestions and shot lists. If you shoot well, editing is easier, faster, and more fun—and the results are a lot more satisfying.

For your first movie, you should choose a simple subject, shoot a variety of shots, and edit them together. What you will then have is a series of edited shots, called a *sequence*. Sequences are like sentences, which become paragraphs when you string them together. Sequences are the basic building blocks of your movies. When you edit a movie, you create it by connecting each sequence to the next sequence.

Making videos is a lot like writing—there's a simple structure that underlies it—and video is a visual language. When you learn how to make sequences and how to make each sequence connect to the next, editing movies becomes easier and faster.

using his camcorder's flip screen to monitor his performance in his video shoots.

He uses free, legally downloadable music and desktop movie editing software to edit his programs. Take a look—and take heart. You can make your own movies, too, in your own home, using the same simple tools as Pogue. And tune in every week for Pogue's latest online movie news on consumer technology, a great free source for the latest tips and tools. You'll learn about new techniques, tools, and sources to enhance your movies.

Some projects may not require any editing at all because they are simple or the cameraperson was talented enough to "edit in the camera." If you learn to shoot well enough, you may not need to do much editing of your footage.

My mentor, Bill Jersey, an acclaimed documentary filmmaker who's shot PBS programs around the world for 35+ years, videotaped my wedding so beautifully that I never had to edit it. Every shot was perfect. He simply turned the camera on when he was ready to shoot something that was happening and turned it off when the sequence was done. It was a great wedding present.

If you learn to shoot well, you, too, can make editing your movies a snap!

Just remember that mastering two simple skills—shooting well and making great sequences—is the goal, and your movies will be not only fun to watch but fast and easy to edit.

Discovering Your Digital Movie Style

Everyone has his or her own style; what's yours? When you shoot and edit your own movies, you should leave yourself room to play and experiment. Don't be afraid to try new things. Try putting yourself on camera, try a new angle—and *watch* what you've shot. Nothing will help you develop your shooting skills more than evaluating what you have shot and how you might shoot it differently next time.

Don't be afraid to make mistakes—after all, you can delete it all! And you can even reuse your tape.

You're *learning*. Give yourself room to discover your own digital movie style.

Digital Movie Gear

To make a movie, you need a camcorder, a personal computer, editing software, and some accessories: an external microphone and extra batteries for your camcorder and, if you like, an external hard drive to use with your computer.

What to Look for in a Digital Video Camcorder

If you already have a digital camcorder, great! If you're in the market for a new one, get a miniDV camcorder, which is a digital video camcorder that records onto miniDV tape.

MiniDV camcorders range in price from $300 to $3,000 and up, but you can generally find a full-featured model for about $300 to $500. Plan to spend more for camera accessories, cables, and perhaps an extra hard drive, which can cost another $300 to $1,000, depending on your budget. You'll find a checklist of recommended items and approximate costs later in this chapter.

In general, compact camcorders cost more than larger models, but the quality of the two types is often about the same. You pay extra for the convenience of having a smaller camera, but some tiny camcorders sacrifice important external connections (such as an external microphone jack). You should get a camera that balances size, weight, features, and your budget, but you shouldn't compromise external connections.

These are some of the essentials your camcorder should have:

- ▶ 10x optical zoom (typical)
- ▶ External microphone input
- ▶ FireWire (also called IEEE 1394 or iLink) connection
- ▶ Image stabilization (helps avoid shaky cam)
- ▶ Low light feature (enables you to shoot at night or in low light)

SHOPPING FOR A CAMCORDER

Don't know which camcorder is for you? CNET has a helpful online movie camcorder buying guide that helps you select the right camera. The guide includes common profiles of camcorder users, including home and vacation movie makers, budget buyers, trendsetters, independent filmmakers, and business videographers.

You can find the CNET digital camcorder buying guide at http://reviews.cnet.com/4520-6500_7-1023271-1.html?tag=fs.

Don't know if digital video is for you? Try this out: For $29.95, you can buy a disposable video camcorder (available at CVS and other outlets) with 20 minutes of shooting time. The quality is comparable to VHS quality (not as good as miniDV), but you can find out if making movies is for you without investing $300 or more.

The disposable camcorder, made by Pure Digital of San Francisco, is about the size of a deck of cards, has easy-to-use controls (On/Off, Playback, Record, and Delete) and weighs about 5 ounces. It has a square, 1.4-inch color LCD screen that is both the viewfinder and playback screen. The camcorder records video to a flash memory card inside the camera.

One minor drawback of the disposable camcorder is that you can see only the last clip you've recorded. It also has no zoom. And it has no image stabilization, which makes it better at close-ups and medium shots than at long shots.

For $12.99, you can get a DVD of your footage from the camera, which you can then import into your computer and edit. Included in this $12.99 purchase is the ability to post your video on the Web and email others with a link to the online movie.

To see an interview with Pure Digital's CEO that was shot with the disposable camcorder, see the San Francisco Chronicle site, at www.sfgate.com/cgi-bin/object/article?f=/chronicle/archive/2005/06/13/BUG00D50EG28.DTL&o=1&type=tech.

▶ Good battery life

▶ Manual controls

In addition, you also want to look for these features:

▶ Top or side tape loading (so you can change tape without removing the camera from a tripod)

▶ Flip screen (so you can see yourself when you shoot yourself)

▶ Remote control (so you control your camcorder if you want to be in your movies while you shoot them)

You might also consider getting a three-chip camcorder, which gives you higher-quality movie recording.

What to Look for in Shooting Accessories and Editing Equipment

Remember that in addition to your camcorder, you need $300 to $1,000 for accessories and perhaps a hard drive for editing. Here is a list of the shooting accessories you should plan to purchase:

▶ **UV filter**—A UV filter protects your valuable camera lens from dust and scratches. This is essential.

▶ **Camera case**—A camera case protects your camcorder and holds your accessories.

▶ **Tripod**—A tripod is a must-have. Some tripods have camera controls so that you can control your camcorder from the tripod handle. Though these cost more, they are *highly* recommended.

▶ **Extra batteries**—Extra batteries extend your shooting time. In general, the basic battery that comes with your camera gives you one hour of shooting time. Buy larger batteries for longer shooting time. Buying two of these longer-lasting batteries is a good way to go. The more batteries you have, the better off you will be.

▶ **Battery charger**—If you want to charge batteries from an outlet or your car, an external battery charger is a good investment.

▶ **External clip-on microphone and cable**—The camcorder-mounted mike that is built in to your camcorder will rarely get good sound. If there's only *one* accessory you can afford to buy (in addition to a UV filter), let it be an external mike. They cost around $20, so this is a great investment.

▶ **Shotgun (or directional) microphone**—If you want to capture audio from a distance without a clip-on mike, you need one of these microphones. They are more expensive than clip-on mikes but capture sound from a larger area.

▶ **FireWire camcorder-to-computer cable**—This connects your camcorder to your computer. Many camcorders come with such a cable, but some do not. You can't edit without one. A FireWire camcorder-to-computer cable is different from the FireWire cable you use to connect your computer to an external hard drive.

▶ **Camera-mounted light**—Some camcorders have a slot for mounting an external light. In general, camera-mounted light is rather harsh and less desirable than other kinds of lighting, but if you must have a light (say, for shooting night interviews), a camera-mounted light would be helpful.

AVOIDING DVD CAMCORDERS

You may be tempted to buy one of the new direct-to-DVD camcorders. These are digital video cameras that record and save your video to DVDs (instead of to miniDV tapes). Don't buy one if you plan to edit most of your movies. Compared to that of a miniDV camcorder, the quality of a DVD camcorder recording is poor; and if you want to edit your footage on your computer, you have to use DVD import software as an extra step in the editing process.

If you use a miniDV camcorder, you can make much higher-quality DVDs, use your computer to quickly and easily edit, and output your movie onto a DVD.

OTHER EQUIPMENT TO CONSIDER

If you're planning to make DVDs, you will need a DVD burner and DVD-burning software. You can find more information about DVD burning software in Chapters 3, "Editing Basics: Movie Maker and More," and 10, "Resources for Learning."

If you're planning to use footage from VHS tapes and you can't connect a VCR to your camcorder, you may have to buy extra cables and hardware for this purpose. You can find more information about importing VHS video in Chapter 9, "Project 5: Making Family Memory Movies."

You'll also need the following editing accessories:

- ▶ **External hard drive**—You will probably need an external hard drive to edit your video. If you are editing only a short amount of video (5 minutes or less), you may have enough room on your computer's hard drive. A larger budget will buy you more hard drive space. In general, prices are about $1 per gigabyte. Many people buy a 200GB to 300GB hard drive for editing video.

- ▶ **FireWire cable**—You need this type of cable to connect an external drive to your computer.

Table 1.1 shows how much you'll need to spend on all these accessories.

TABLE 1.1 Shooting Accessories and Editing Equipment Budget			
	Low	Medium	High
Shooting Accessories			
UV filter to protect camera lens	$15	$15	$15
Camera case	$30	$50	$100
Tripod	$50	$150	$150
Extra battery (4 hour)		$80	$80
Battery charger			$80
External clip-on mike (and battery)	$20	$20	$20
External mike cable	$15	$15	$15
FireWire cable (camcorder-to-computer)	$30	$30	$30
A second extra battery (4 hour)			$80
Shotgun/directional mike			$100
Camera-mounted light			$80
Subtotal (shooting accessories)	**$160**	**$360**	**$750**

TABLE 1.1 Continued			
	Low	**Medium**	**High**
Editing Equipment			
External hard drive	$125	$225	$275
FireWire cable (external drive to computer)	$30	$30	$30
Subtotal (editing accessories)	**$155**	**$255**	**$305**
Total (all accessories)	**$315**	**$615**	**$1,055**

Movie Editing Software and Computer Requirements

Most PC owners have a free desktop movie editing software program built into their computer: Movie Maker from Microsoft. Chapters 3 and 4 describe how to use Movie Maker to edit and share your movies. Because Movie Maker is free, it's one of the most popular programs for movie editing. If you are willing to purchase your own editing software, you can choose from many other options, many of which offer special features, such as DVD burning capabilities (which Movie Maker does not provide). See Chapter 10 for descriptions and information on how to get free, downloadable trial versions of other editing programs.

Macintosh owners generally use the free software iMovie HD from Apple or Final Cut, a professional software program. iMovie is part of the iLife suite and is packaged on most Apple computers; it's also available for purchase at www.apple.com. The following section discusses the computer requirements for using Movie Maker because that's the most

ON A TIGHT BUDGET?

Want to see whether digital video is for you without spending a bundle? If you can't borrow a camcorder from someone, or if you just want to play around before investing in a camcorder, here are low- or no-cost ways you can shoot, edit, and share movies:

▸ **Make family memory movies (free)**—If you have scanned or digital photos or old home movies that have been digitized, you can make a family memory movie at virtually no cost on your personal computer with Movie Maker (which is free). See Chapter 9 for more information.

▸ **Shoot 20 minutes with a disposable camcorder ($30)**—Using a disposable camcorder, you can shoot 20 minutes of VHS-quality video, and for $12.99 more, you can save your video to a DVD or share it on the Web. It's a little complicated to edit it on your computer, but you may be able to import the footage from the DVD, if you purchased one. For more information, see the sidebar "Disposable Camcorders" in this chapter and check the latest information available from the manufacturer's or seller's website.

▸ **Buy a used camcorder (variable)**—Many people are selling miniDV camcorders on eBay and www.craigslist.org. You can often buy a used camcorder at a great price; some camcorders on eBay still even carry warranties.

▸ **Get free editing software**—Many editing software companies offer free, 30-day trials of their editing software, which you can download from the Web. These programs provide more features than Movie Maker,

continues

including the ability to burn DVDs. See Chapter 10 for more information.

▸ **Share your movies online (free)—You can use Neptune's Mediashare service (Microsoft's video hosting partner) free for a three-day trial period. Other movie hosting services (sites that save and play your movies online) are available for free, with no time limits. See Chapter 4, "Saving and Sharing Digital Movies," for more information.**

With a $300 camcorder and tapes that costs $10 for an hour's worth of video, you can shoot a lot of video. For the same money, you would pay to see 34 Hollywood movies. If you use your camcorder a lot, that's great entertainment value for the money.

widely available software for movie editing. (If you don't have Movie Maker on your computer, you can download it for free from the Microsoft website at http:/// www.microsoft.com/windowsxp/downloads/ updates/moviemaker2.mspx.)

Movie Maker Computer Requirements

In order to capture and edit digital video from your camcorder, you need the following *minimum* system configuration (required by Microsoft to run Movie Maker):

▸ Windows XP Home Edition (with Service Pack 2) or Windows XP Professional

▸ 600MHz processor (Intel Pentium III, AMD Athlon, or equivalent)

▸ 128MB of RAM

▸ 2GB of available hard disk space

While these are the minimum requirements, if your computer just meets these specs, it will run very slowly, and you may be very frustrated. You'll be much happier if you have the following configuration (which Microsoft *recommends*):

▸ 1.5GHz processor (Intel Pentium 4, AMD Athlon XP 1500+, or equivalent)

▸ 256MB of RAM

In addition, you need the following:

▸ An external hard drive, unless your videos are very short (5 minutes or less)

▸ A digital video capture card (included on most newer PCs and also available from other manufacturers)

▸ A FireWire port on your computer

Summary

In this chapter, you've learned that millions of people like you are creating their own digital movies. To get started, you just need a camcorder, the right accessories, your personal computer, and free editing software.

Now that you know what gear you need to have, you can get it all together and start learning about the two essential skills you need to develop—shooting and editing—in the next two chapters.

Ready to learn about shooting? Turn the page.

WATCHING MOVIES ONLINE

Want to get some online inspiration? Many of the big search sites on the Internet have launched movie services where you can find thousands of online movies to watch—many from major media outlets. For example, AOL has more than 15,000 professional, high-quality movies from Time Warner on its site. Here are some of the top choices:

- Google—http://video.google.com/video_about.html
- Yahoo!—http://video.yahoo.com
- MSN—http://video.msn.com/video/p.htm
- AOL—www.aol.com
- Blinkx—www.Blinkx.tv

In addition, you can find lots of fun movies online at some of the sites that specialize in independent films and shorts, including www.atomfilms.com.

CHAPTER 2

Shooting Digital Movies

In this chapter, you'll learn how to shoot great video. First we'll cover the basics: shot types, sequences, action, and directing. Then, using two top 10 lists, we'll review camcorder and shooting essentials. More than anything else, making videos means shooting well. What makes a movie wonderful to watch? These are some of the most common elements:

▶ Stable shots

▶ Shots that last 5 to 15 seconds

▶ A variety of shots (long, medium, and close-up)

▶ Good audio

When you shoot well, you may hardly have to edit at all—or, at least, your editing task will be much, much easier. So, let's find out how to shoot, using the basic shot types, and then cover the basic features on your camcorder and how to work with your shooting environment so you can make great movies.

Using What You Already Know

Many people are already familiar with taking digital photos. Shooting movies uses many of the same principles of composition and lighting. But there are a few techniques that are new for most people who are already familiar with photography: recording action, getting high-quality audio, and creating sequences.

Using what you already knows means you can put to work everything you know from watching the thousands of hours of television shows and movies you've probably seen. While most people don't usually pay too much attention to how movies and films are constructed, there is a lot of visual grammar that you probably already know but may not have thought much about—until now.

So here's a suggestion: The next time you see a television program or movie, notice how long each shot lasts, how often the camera moves, and how the shots are edited together.

To focus your attention on the visuals alone, try watching a show without the audio. Analyze the shots and how they are edited together, and you'll see that series of shots edited together—called *sequences*—provide the basic building blocks in the edited footage.

Shots and Sequences: The Building Blocks of Movies

When you watch television or DVDs, you see that in general, the camera doesn't really move that much. Instead, series of individual static shots are edited together into sequences, much as we use words to make sentences. In a way, movies aren't that different from slideshows, except that instead of using still photos, movies use moving images.

Sequences are made up of a variety of shots, usually framed in different sizes or from different points of view. These shots are fairly standardized into three main types: long, wide (establishing) shots; medium shots; and close-up shots.

In creating your own movies, you'll want to record footage of these different types of shots to make into sequences when you edit your movie.

When you watch a movie, try to see how often sequences are created using the three basic types of shots:

- **Long shot, wide shot, or establishing shot**—A *long*, or *wide*, *shot*, also called an *establishing shot*, is a broad shot that shows "the big picture" and helps viewers locate the scene in time and space. It can be the exterior of a house, the outside of a building, or a landscape. It might be two or three characters walking together on a street or getting in and out of cars. There is often no dialog in this type of shot.

- **Medium shot**—A *medium shot* is from a person's waist up and tells you more about the person and less about the space. It gives much more visual information about the person and can often include audio with the person.

- **Close-up shot**—A *close up shot* is generally of the head and shoulders. A close-up is used in narrative films for dialogue and for more intimate information about the subject. In interviews, the camera often switches back and forth between medium and close-up shots.

In addition, you may also see these two types of shots:

- **Full shot**—A *full shot* is of a whole person and is used to tell more about the person in the context of his or her environment.

- **Extreme close-up shot**—An *extreme close-up shot* is a shot of the face and neck. It provides a very intimate feeling of the person and his or her emotions or words.

MOVIES TO INSPIRE YOU

Want to know more about shooting? While a book can tell you many things, seeing movie-making techniques onscreen is helpful in illustrating visual material about lighting and shooting.

The two DVDs *The Young Filmmakers Club: Video Camera Techniques* and *Visions of Light: The Art of Cinematography* span the alpha and omega of shooting. *The Young Filmmakers Club: Video Camera Techniques* (25 minutes), narrated by child actor Logan O'Brien, is, in fact, not just for kids! It's so easy to understand, with a good overview of equipment and techniques, that it will help any video beginner learn a lot. It covers how to use your camcorder, tripod shooting, handheld shooting, composing your shots, and more. A plus is that it also covers some of the more subtle elements of filmmaking—such as what the subtext of a subject facing left in the frame implies, for instance—that are nice to know and rarely found in movie how-to shows. For more information, visit www.youngfilmmakersclub.com.

Visions of Light (95 minutes) is an extraordinary, full-length feature documentary that has dazzled and delighted audiences with behind-the-scenes stories and captivating footage from the making of more than 125 famous films. "*Visions of Light* is not just for film buffs," writes Amazon.com's reviewer, and I agree.

The film covers cinematography and cinematographers from D.W. Griffith's *Birth of a Nation* to the modern thriller *Blade Runner*, and it takes you inside production sets and studios to show you how critical scenes were lit and how action was orchestrated, from light to shadow. After you've seen *Visions of Light*, the next time you go to a movie, you'll have a much deeper appreciation for the care and skill that go into lighting and cinematography.

Examples of Shot Types

The following figures show some shots that illustrate the different feelings and information you get from a wide shot, a medium shot, and a close-up. These are from an Easter party movie I made of my godson Henry and his two friends.

Figure 2.1 shows a wide shot. In this wide shot, we see that the action is taking place in a yard and that there are three children in the space, holding Easter baskets.

Figure 2.2 shows a medium shot. In this medium shot, we see two children in more detail than in the wide shot, and we get more information about what they are wearing and what they are doing. Compared to the wide shot, in this shot, we don't see as much visual information about where the children are, but we can see more of the activity they are engaged in, as well as some expression on their faces.

In the close-up shot shown in Figure 2.3, we see facial expression very well, but we don't know who is sitting near the subject (as in the medium shot) or the space in which the subject is seated (as in the wide shot). The close-up tells us more about what the subject is feeling and establishes an intimate connection between the subject and the viewer.

For each movie that you shoot, you can use the three basic shot types—long, medium, and close-up—to capture what is happening. The best movies use a variety of these three types of shots.

You can switch between these different shot types two ways: by changing the framing of the shot from the position you are already in (moving the camera lens) or by moving your-self (and your camera) to a different position.

When you understand that it usually takes more than one type of shot to create a

FIGURE 2.1

A wide shot.

sequence, you'll see that you need to get a variety of shots. You need to shoot a lot to get good coverage.

Because shooting video is a bit different from the way people shoot still photographs, it may take awhile for the concepts of shots and sequences to sink in, so don't worry about getting it" right away. Just watch more television and movies and let your awareness and attention on shots and sequences grow.

FIGURE 2.2

A medium shot.

FIGURE 2.3

A close-up shot.

Feature films, commercials, and music videos all begin life in *storyboards*—a series of scenes drawn by an artist to show the flow of shots the production will capture. A storyboard looks like a cartoon strip, and it helps everyone see how sequences will be constructed—before they are shot.

Storyboards are great for learning about how to think about sequences, and they can certainly be very useful in visualizing any kind of movie project.

If you are beginning to shoot and want to think through a movie by storyboarding, you can use a number of resources to learn more.

Here are some websites that feature free storyboarding visualization tools and resources:

▸ Dependent Films—Dependent Films has dozens of free goodies in "Tools and Utilities for Filmmakers," including three different free downloadable storyboard forms. You'll find budget forms, release forms, editing logs, and much more. Visit www.dependent-films.net/files.html.

▸ Atomic Learning—This movie tutorial website offers Storyboard Pro, which is free downloadable software for creating storyboards. You'll also find a free online movie tutorial, "Video Storytelling Guide," which is a series of 16 short online movies designed to help you learn how to explain the "grammar" of filmmaking. See www.atomiclearning.com/storyboardpro.

▸ The Storyboard Artist—Storyboard artist Josh Sheppard has a great website (see Figure 2.4) with dozens of examples of his storyboards for commercials, TV, and feature films, as well as a free online

Action and Directing

Another way that filmmaking differs from picture taking is *action*. While you can just walk up to any scene and snap a photo, movies take place in time. And time changes everything.

While you can make a good movie about many things, in general, movies are full of action and people. And, as you will discover, making movies of people is quite different from taking photographs of them. They usually do and say things on video, which is one of the things that makes it quite wonderful—and one of the things that makes movie making a challenge.

You can control the flow of action by directing your movies.

Directing

Directing a movie means, at the most basic level, being thoughtful about arranging or recording action. It doesn't necessarily mean telling people what to do; but it does mean making choices about what to put on camera—from the action you choose to record to the type of shot you select for each action.

All those reality shows and PBS documentaries that you thought were totally unscripted? Well, they weren't—and yet they were. The reality shows? The filmmakers created scenes that naturally had drama built into them. The documentaries? The filmmakers researched possible interviewees and subjects and carefully edited a series of compelling interactions with people, places, or animals.

The point is that none of these shows was the result of just aimlessly wandering around or hanging out—and they all involved interacting with people. Interacting with people is also known as *directing*, and most of the best movies were created because a director orchestrated a series of interactions with people on camera, choosing the appropriate type of shot (long, medium, or close-up) for each interaction.

Directing a documentary (by *documentary*, I mean any movie that is not a narrative, scripted movie) ranges from asking your 3-year-old to stand where the light is to interviewing your 90-year-old great-grandmother about her nut bread recipe. It means shaping the free flow of people and life into moments on camera that capture life in its unfolding.

Directing a documentary doesn't mean putting a rigid box on life and trying to make non-actors act. It is a balancing act of making a movie while being in the flow, and it takes a little getting used to. When you get the hang of it, you'll see that it's a natural process much like taking a photograph, but slightly more complex.

The project chapters in this book—Chapters 5, "Project 1: Creating Birthday Party and New Baby Movies," through 9, "Project 5: Making Family Memory Movies"—show you how to direct different kinds of documentaries. These chapters provide lots of inspiration, tips, and advice on how to direct movies for specific kinds of situations. Each situation calls for specific technical and creative considerations, which are covered in detail.

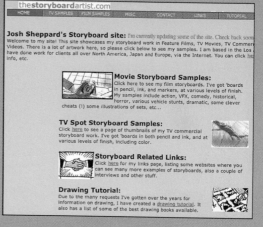

FIGURE 2.4

The Storyboard Artist website.

tutorial about making storyboards. See www.storyboardartist.com.

▸ *Storyboard* magazine—The French publication *Storyboard* magazine is dedicated to international coverage of storyboard artists and their work. You can read it at www.storyboard.fr, using Google's French-to-English translation. Go to Google and type in Storyboard Fr and click Translate. This Page on the Google search results page, which then takes you to the site and provides the text in English. The site features hundreds of online interviews with storyboard artists from Japan, Europe, and the United States.

PRACTICING BEING INVISIBLE

What does being invisible mean?

In terms of audio, it means unless you are in your movie on camera, you won't be in the movie. That means that comments you make probably won't be part of your movie, so don't make sounds unless you plan to edit them out (or you *want* them included). Don't let your unwanted sounds overlap with other sounds you want to have in your movie.

In terms of visuals, being invisible means you may not want the people in the movie to be looking at the camera. If you're taping a business presentation, and you shoot a shot of the audience, you want the audience to be looking at the speaker, not at you. So work with people, or shoot long enough so that they no longer look at the camera but go about their normal business. (In some cases, you do want the subjects looking right into the camera, so you don't need to follow this advice.)

When you're invisible, it's easier to shoot people interacting with other people on camera. They have someone to relate to other than the "invisible" but-in-real-life-clearly-visible you.

Being invisible takes a little figuring out, but it's really not that hard. It may feel a little unnatural, but you will learn how to curb your social instincts in order to meet the demands of shooting and how to coach your subjects to get the best on-camera results.

In some case, you might want to just be visible. Of course, for lots of informal movies, it's perfectly wonderful for you to be off-camera and talking to someone on camera or for people to look at the camera. Just know what you want so you can be sure that's what you get.

Audio

Another big difference between shooting pictures and shooting video is audio. If only your camera-mounted microphone could capture sound as well as your lens captures light. But that's just one more thing that keeps videotaping interesting: It's full of little challenges.

If you want good audio, you have to put a mike where the sound you want is (or, at the very least, you have to point a shotgun, or directional, mike toward it). This is not a natural, intuitive thing that most human beings understand right away.

Cameras work so well from a distance, so why doesn't audio work the same way? That is just the way things are. You have to be much more accommodating in the world of audio than in the world of video. But luckily, humans have invented a marvelous array of audio devices to capture sound, which gives you a chance to buy more fabulous gear! Fortunately, even a $20 investment in an external clip-on mike will get you good sound.

If you want good audio, you'll have to use external microphones to get the mike where the sound you want is. Your camera will also have to be connected to the external microphone with an audio extension cord (unless you have an expensive radio mike).

A basic clip-on microphone (see Figures 2.5 and 2.6) lets you capture sound close to the source rather than using the microphone built into your camcorder. Clip-on microphones come in two pieces—a clip and the microphone. Generally, you can use the clip to hold the microphone and attach the clip to your

FIGURE 2.5

External clip-on microphone (clip and microphone).

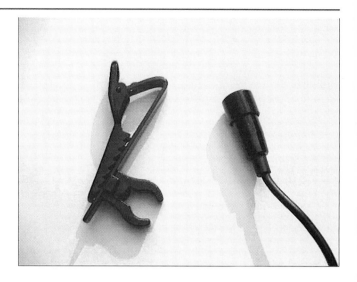

FIGURE 2.6

External clip-on microphone (assembled).

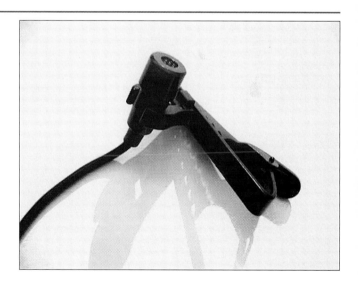

subject's clothing, although you could mount the microphone on almost anything.

A clip-on mike is great for pinning on someone's clothing and getting audio from a single source. Other types of commonly used microphones are the shotgun, or directional, microphones and the rarer omnidirectional microphones.

A shotgun, or directional, mike (which can be mounted on your camera) records audio from a narrow sector of space (that's why it's called *directional*), rather than all the noise in a room, for instance. Most of the sidewalk interviews you see on TV news are recorded with a shotgun, or directional, mike which makes it easier to hear the speakers than the surrounding noise.

If you want all the noise in the room (or street), you need to use an omnidirectional mike, which gathers sound equally from all directions.

Shotgun, or directional, mikes are much more commonly used than omnidirectional mikes, but because they usually cost more than clip-on mikes, they tend to be used in interviewing more than one person or when you don't want to be connected by a cord from your camera to the subject.

I can't emphasize enough how important it is to get good audio. While it seems like extra work, taking a few minutes to get people properly miked makes the difference between a movie that's not very fun to watch and one that's riveting.

If you want to understand what a difference microphones make, do a simple test: Record your subject from 6 to 10 feet away, using your camera's microphone. Then record the same subject and audio with a clip-on microphone. Compare the two and listen to the difference yourself. Which one would you rather hear?

Top 10 Camera Essentials

Before you begin shooting, it's important to learn about your camcorder. You need to take time to get acquainted with it. After all, you'll be spending a lot of time together.

You don't have to read the camcorder manual from cover to cover, but you do need to know a few of the camera's most basic functions. Of course, over time, you may decide that reading the camcorder manual is much more exciting than you would have guessed! (That's when you know you're hooked.) Your manual has a lot to tell you about this powerful piece of equipment.

The following sections describe the top 10 fundamental functions you need to learn.

1. On/Off

You should find out where the On/Off power button is and learn how to use it.

2. Record/Standby

Record/Standby is generally a red button on your camcorder that you push to start. When you're powered up, you see a signal on your camcorder that you are in standby mode. When you push the Record button, the signal turns to red, and you're recording. Push the same button again, and you are in standby mode.

3. Widen/Tighten

The Widen and Tighten controls are usually labeled W and T. You use these controls to zoom the camera lens in and out. You need to find out how the W/T rocker bar or controller works and then avoid the temptation to use it while you are recording. Constantly zooming in and out is one of the most obvious, irritating, and often repeated sign of a bad home movie!

4. Inserting Tape

You need to find out how to load tape into your camcorder. Do not force the tape loading mechanism. It is very delicate—and it is very expensive to fix if you break it. I have done this, so I speak from experience.

5. Autofocus and Manual Focus

Most cameras have autofocus, which is a wonderful feature for many situations, but sometimes it can get in the way. Often, the only manual control you should really get to know is manual focus, so you can choose when you want to use autofocus and when you want manual focus. (You'll learn more about manual focus later in this chapter.)

6. Batteries

You need to find the feature on your camcorder that tells you how much battery life is in your camera batteries. And you need to learn how to charge the batteries. If you have extra batteries or a separate battery charger, you should make sure you can charge them. And you should find out how long it takes to charge them, too.

7. Camera Case

It is important to keep your camera in a case and protect it from extreme temperatures and moisture. Keeping your camera in a nice, protected camera case is a very good way to protect your investment. You can also store all your accessories with it in the case, so you will be ready to shoot at a moment's notice.

TAPE HANDLING AND ORGANIZING TIPS

While it may sound too trivial to talk about at first, handling tapes is actually a pretty important part of the process of shooting a movie. So it's worth a minute of your time to review these basic tape handling and organizing tips:

▸ **Unwrap tapes**—It's a good idea to unwrap tapes *before* you need them so you're not frantically trying to remove the cellophane wrapper when you want to be shooting. It's no fun to miss the important action because you are stuck trying to get your fingernail under that pesky wrapper that just won't come off quickly.

In addition, unwrapping the cellophane wrapper makes noise, and if you're in the middle of a school concert, the rest of the audience will not enjoy the "sounds of cellophane" symphony you've introduced into the program. Be polite and unwrap tapes before the event begins. Unwrapping during an interview also creates an interruption in the flow of a taping session; it's bad enough to have to change tape, so minimize your tape change time by having tapes ready to load if you think your first tape is going to run out.

▸ **Label tapes**—It's a good idea to label tapes so you know what's what. You can even pre-label tapes if you are getting ready for a shoot; professionals often do this. You don't want to have to shuffle through tape after tape when you go to edit your tapes because you didn't label them. Sometimes you don't get around to editing your footage until long after the shoot. You'll be shuffling around enough footage for real editing

continues

work; don't make extra work for yourself by not labeling your tapes.

▸ **Use the Record/Save tab**—You need to learn about and find the Record/Save tab on your tapes. This is the black slider near the tape edge of the miniDV cassette tape. The tape comes ready for recording, with the Record/Tab slider in the Record position. You need to push the tab to the opposite side after you've finished shooting to prevent it from being erased or recorded over. You should get in the habit of pushing this tab when you take tape out of the camera. If you've ever recorded over a precious event tape, you know just how heartbreaking it can be to lose valuable footage.

▸ **Make "lock and label" your motto**—You should *lock* the tape's Save tab and *label* your tape—*every time* you take a tape out of the camcorder. If it becomes automatic, you won't have to worry about losing the footage you've shot—at least not for a really preventable reason.

You should store your camcorder and your tapes in a cool, dry place. Don't leave your camera in the car for months at a time, in a hot or cold climate, thinking you'll have it in case you need it right away. Aside from preventing theft, you need to keep it safe from extreme temperatures.

8. Tripod

If you have a tripod, you should put the camera on the tripod and practice using it. If you have a tripod with camera controls on the tripod handle, you should practice using the controls on the tripod handle to control your camera.

9. External Microphone

If you have an external microphone, you need to learn how it connects to your camcorder and test it. You should make sure the microphone battery is working properly and carry an extra battery in your camera case at all times.

10. White Balance

In your camcorder manual, you should find the section about white-balancing your camera. What is white balancing? Your camcorder reads white and then calculates all the other colors from it. The camera has to find white in the scene it sees.

Shooting under incandescent light (which makes images yellowish/orangey) or fluorescent light (which casts a blue tinge on images) changes the color temperature of the light, so what should be white is not read by the camera as white.

Top 10 Tips for Shooting Video

Finally, you're ready to shoot. Life is happening, and you're raring to scoop it up. Have gear, will go! You've learned about the three basic kinds of shots, you understand what it takes to create sequences, and you know how to use your camcorder. Now you're going out to give it your best. You're visualizing the wonderful movie you'll make. And you're ready to get the best footage to make your editing a snap!

Here's a list of the top 10 things you need to know to have a great shoot.

1. Use a Tripod As Often As You Can

Why, you ask, would you want to use a tripod? Well, try shooting some footage without a tripod and then shooting the same scene with one. Look at the results. Which version would you rather watch? Unless you're a world-class cinematographer who's mastered the art of handheld shooting over years, you'll probably want to watch the footage you shot on the tripod.

The human eye is sensitive to motion, and we feel much more comfortable when things are steady, as they (usually) are in the real world. Remember to bring and use a tripod (or a monopod) on your video adventures, and your movies will be much, much better to watch.

Like videos that zoom in and out too often, shaky, handheld shots are one of the most common mistakes beginners make in shooting videos. You don't make yourself concentrate on learning how to hold the camera steady when you can leave that job to your tripod and focus your attention on more important aspects of your shoot. Free yourself—use a tripod!

If you can't bring a tripod, look for natural objects to use as tripods. Things like fences, chairs, big rocks, a ski pole, and a car hood all make good stable platforms.

If you make a tripod your constant companion, your shooting and your movies will be better for it.

2. Learn How to Shoot Stable Handheld Shots

There are some times when using a tripod is impractical or impossible. Only in those cases should you take handheld shots. To shoot well, brace the camera against your body in a way that's comfortable for you. Practice this. Watch the video you shoot. You can also lean against objects in your environment to help you steady yourself and your camera.

As you get better, you can try walking with the camera while you shoot. Walk slowly and deliberately, while holding the camera against your body. Again, watch your footage. You can practice this over time and see how your skill increases.

If you plan to walk and shoot often, you might want to learn more about the common camera shoulder braces and equipment that can make walking and shooting much easier. These cost about $150 and up for a miniDV camcorder. Professional models start at $700. Learning how to shoot handheld shots will also give you new appreciation for the skill of professionals when you see those shots on TV.

3. Avoid Frequent Panning and Zooming

Panning is moving a shot from side to side. *Zooming* is using the camera lens to move closer to and farther from the subject. One of the common mistakes beginners make is zooming and panning too often and too fast.

Why? No one knows, really, but it's so common that there must be a reason. Maybe it's because there's that Widen/Tighten button on your camcorder, and you feel like doing something rather than just standing there. Learning how to just stand there is a new skill you'll come to enjoy. Because you're not just standing there—you're shooting great video!

Of course, you can pan and zoom, but use these controls slowly and sparingly. Watch TV and see how few zooms and pans you see. You will generally see pans and zooms used very, very subtly or for some very good reason.

Panning and zooming can be very effective, but *only* when done *slowly* and generally with a tripod. When you are getting set up for a new shot, you may pan or zoom just to change your framing and your shot before the action continues.

4. Hold Your Shot

Another common mistake is not having a long enough shot. While you may use only 5 to 15 seconds in your edited program, you want to make sure that the focus is not changing during your shot, that there is no panning or zooming, and that you have enough extra footage on the ends of your edited shots to insert cross-dissolves or other transitions.

As a general rule, let each shot run at least 10 to 20 seconds or more.

5. Shoot a Lot

One of the secrets of making great movies is to shoot a lot. As one saying goes, "shoot relentlessly and edit ruthlessly."

Shooting a lot means getting lots of coverage. Remember that when you edit your footage, you will use only the best shots. You'll be *very* selective *then*—but not when you're shooting.

Tape is cheap. Shoot what attracts you. Tape several takes. If you videotape several takes, when you edit, you're more likely to find that one is better than the others. If in doubt, play a take back in the camera. But don't be afraid to shoot several takes.

In a typical documentary, it's common to shoot 10 times more tape than the length of the finished program—and that was true even in the days of film, when it cost a lot to shoot. So don't be surprised if you shoot 10 hours to edit a 1-hour movie or 1 hour of tape to make a 5-minute movie. You may, of course, shoot more than 10:1—and that would probably be a good thing.

6. Get Good Audio

After too much panning and zooming, and shaky cam (from not using a tripod) poor audio is one of the most common beginners' mistakes. One reason is the poor quality of a built-in camera microphone—and its location.

If you use only a camera mike, count on shooting a lot of medium or close-up shots or putting music over your movies from beginning to end.

To see how much better the audio is with a clip-on mike, try this experiment: Shoot a subject in a quiet room with your camera mike. Then shoot the subject with the clip-on mike. Hear the difference?

Use external microphones to get better audio.

7. Leave Headroom

Always leave a comfortable amount of headroom above your subject's head. *Headroom* is the space between the top of the subject's head and the movie frame.

If headroom is cramped, your subject will look squeezed in your movie and make viewers uncomfortable. If you leave too much headroom, your subject will appear smaller than people are used to seeing subjects in a movie. Watch television to see how professionals frame their head shots and try to shoot with a comfortable amount of space above your subject's head.

For most people, this will comes fairly naturally. Just think of how you would take a photograph of someone's head and frame your movie the same way.

8. Know When to Use Manual Focus

Most of the time, you can use the autofocus on your camcorder. It's great when your subject is not moving. But if someone else walks into your shot, autofocus then tries to put that person in focus, which is not necessarily what you want. On the other hand, if you're shooting fast motion—like a sports game—you should use your autofocus because it can focus

faster than you can manually. Experiment to see how the different focus options work and what works best under different conditions.

9. Compose Your Shots

There is a commonly used formula called the *rule of thirds* that artists and camera people use as a guideline for composing interesting visuals. The rule of thirds says you should divide the screen into a grid that has two horizontal lines and two vertical lines—like a tic tac toe board. You should try to put your subject off-center, to make your shots more complex and interesting.

10. Watch Your Lighting

Like audio, lighting is a tricky bit to learn when you start shooting video. Everyone says "avoid backlighting," and that's good advice, but there's much more than that to lighting. It's not easy to make things look great without using lights to light your scene, but you can do the best you can with the conditions you have. Here are a few pointers:

- ▶ Look for the best light in a situation and ask your subjects to stand there—under a tree, for instance, where it's not too shady, but not as bright as glaring sunlight.
- ▶ Shoot with light on someone's face rather than light coming from behind the person.
- ▶ Try to avoid high-contrast light situations.
- ▶ If you're shooting indoors, you may need to turn on every light in the room in order to get enough light everywhere.
- ▶ Many cameras come with a low-light mode for shooting night scenes. Find out where this feature is and how to turn this control on if you are going to be shooting

in a low-light situation. Compare what your footage looks like with and without using the low-light mode to better understand the difference.

Remember: Your lighting doesn't have to be perfect. It just needs to be as good as you can make it under the circumstances you're shooting in.

TIP

Want to get up to speed on lighting? Check out "Light Right—A Crash Course in Lighting Video," by John Jackman, at www.techlearning.com/story/showArticle.jhtml?articleID=12800456.

Summary

In this chapter, you've learned about some of the key concepts in shooting movies: shot types, sequences, action, and directing. You've gotten hands-on, practical information about your camcorder and how to use it, and you've learned how to avoid many of the common mistakes beginners make: not using a tripod, zooming and panning a lot, and getting poor audio. You've learned about the right way to shoot—using long, medium, and close-up shots—how to handle tape, and how to be invisible when the occasion calls for it.

In this chapter you've also discovered resources to help you visualize movies before you start shooting as well as resources to inspire and delight you.

Now you're ready for the second basic skill you need to learn: how to edit.

CHAPTER 3

Editing Basics: Movie Maker and More

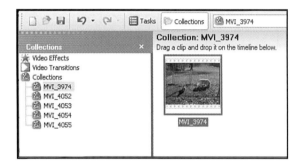

Now that you've shot your video, you can get started with the all-important task of learning how to edit your video into a movie.

Editing video is a lot like editing a slideshow—but with a few new twists. This chapter covers the following:

- **A tour of Movie Maker**—You'll discover the basic functions and learn about the interface (without having to know how to use the program yet).

- **A hands-on Movie Maker exercise**—With detailed step-by-step instructions, you'll learn how to edit a few clips (and music and photos, if you have them) together for a beginning exercise. (You can use these same instructions in your ongoing video editing, simply expanding the number of video clips and other material.)

- **Top 10 tips for editing your video**—Editing involves more than knowing how your editing software works. In this chapter you'll learn about the creative aspects of editing and the importance of audio and music.

- **How to use effects and titles and where to find music and sound effects**—In this chapter you'll learn how to use video effects, learn how to use titles to structure and liven up your movie, and learn where to go for free or low-cost music and sound effects downloads that can add more life and energy to your movies.

- **Editing inspiration**—A sidebar on DVDs about TV and film editors introduces entertaining programs that take you inside the editing process.

In addition to what you learn here, in Chapter 10, "Resources for Learning," you'll learn more about upgrading your editing skills (with a list

of popular Movie Maker websites) and other, more full-featured editing software available on the market. Many of the editing programs are available for free trial and include DVD-burning software (which is not part of Movie Maker). You can go to Chapter 10 now to get Web addresses for free trial downloads if you're interested in trying out more complete tools. If you use a tool other than Movie Maker, you'll still find the top 10 editing tips list and sidebar resources in this chapter very useful.

Are you ready for a tour of Movie Maker? Let's get an overview of the program, and then we'll jump into how to edit your first video clips.

Getting Acquainted with Movie Maker: The Grand Tour

This overview tour of Movie Maker is *only a* tour. It is designed to help you get the big picture of what's available in Movie Maker. You'll find that Movie Maker is actually pretty easy to use. If you have put together a slideshow using your computer, you'll see that the process of using Movie Maker isn't that much different—except that you have the added elements of motion and audio.

After the tour, we'll get back to basics and focus on only the easy, simple, essential steps of making your first movie. So relax and enjoy the tour!

The Movie Tasks pane is the engine room of Movie Maker, and it's where you'll do most tasks, so you should focus on learning how it works, and then you'll be ahead of the game.

As with most software programs, there are multiple ways to access features in Movie Maker. You can use the Movie Tasks pane for most of your work; it's the easiest way to get around in Movie Maker. That's the approach we'll take to navigating in Movie Maker. Before we dive in to the tour, here's a list of the basic steps of using Movie Maker, which this chapter covers in detail:

1. Finding and opening Movie Maker

2. Connecting your camcorder to your computer

3. Importing your video (and photos, if you are using any)

4. Editing your video

5. Inserting transitions

6. Adding music (optional)

7. Saving your movie (covered in Chapter 4, "Saving and Sharing Digital Movies")

Finding Movie Maker

If you have Windows XP, you'll find Movie Maker already loaded on your computer. If you don't already have Movie Maker, or you can download a free copy of Movie Maker from Microsoft.com's Movie Maker website (www.microsoft.com/windowsxp/downloads/updates/moviemaker2.mspx). Then you need to follow the Setup Wizard steps to install the software.

> **NOTE**
>
> To review the list of computer requirements for Movie Maker, refer to the section "Movie Maker Computer Requirements" in Chapter 1, "Welcome to the Wonderful World of Digital Video," or see the Microsoft website www.microsoft.com/windowsxp/downloads/updates/moviemaker2.mspx.

Opening Movie Maker

After you have installed Movie Maker, you open the program by selecting Start, All Programs, Windows Movie Maker (see Figure 3.1).

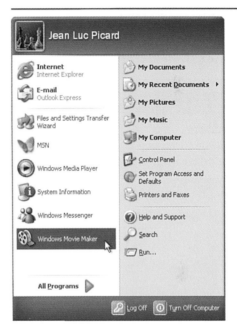

FIGURE 3.1
Opening Movie Maker.

> **NOTE**
>
> If you don't find Movie Maker under All Programs, look under All Programs, Accessories, Entertainment, and you should find it there.

Exploring Movie Maker

Now we'll go through each of the areas of Movie Maker so you can see what each of them does.

We'll look at the menu and the toolbar, and then we'll explore the rest of the Movie Maker interface, which includes the Movie Tasks pane, the Collections pane, and the Storyboard and Timeline views.

The Menu

Let's explore the menu commands at the top of the screen, starting with the File menu options. You can highlight each one to see what's underneath it:

- **File**—The File menu is the where you can access projects and capture and import video clips.

- **Edit**—The Edit menu is where you can perform basic editing functions.

- **View**—The View menu controls the different views of Movie Maker functions.

- **Tools**—The Tools menu is where you access titles, credits, effects, transitions, and audio levels.

- **Clip**—You use the Clip menu to trim your clips and perform other functions.

- **Play**—The Play menu moves your clips forward and backward—frame-by-frame, as a clip, or as a storyboard.

- **Help**—The Help menu shows you where to get help for all of Movie Maker's features and provides links to online resources at the Microsoft website.

The Toolbar

Below the menus is the toolbar, shown in Figure 3.2, which provides shortcuts for many of the menus we've just explored. If you've used Word, for instance, many of the shortcuts in the toolbar will seem familiar—Save, Undo, Redo, and so on. The buttons Tasks and

Collections let you shift easily between those two views.

The Movie Tasks Pane

On the left of your screen is a section titled Movie Tasks. This is the Movie Tasks pane, which is so easy to use that you don't really need to use the menu or the toolbar often.

As shown in Figure 3.3, the Movie Tasks pane is divided into three main categories—Capture Video, Edit Movie, and Finish Movie—plus an onscreen help section called Movie Making Tips.

To see what's available within each of the three main categories, you can click the arrows beside the titles. For example, you can see all the listings under Capture Video in Figure 3.3. To see the similar listing of tasks available under Edit Movie, you click the downward-pointing arrow to the right of Edit Movie.

The Collections Pane

The center of the Movie Maker screen is the Collections pane, where you can see the video clips you've selected from your collections (see Figure 3.4). Movie Maker stores your clips in collections, and over time, you will see more and more filenames under this option when you click it. The Collections pane also shows video effects and transitions.

You can access the same information you see at the left in the Collections pane more efficiently by using the drop-down toolbar menu items to display collections. This shows all the same information but leaves the Movie Tasks pane visible as well, so you can navigate more easily to more of the features you use often.

FIGURE 3.2

The Movie Maker toolbar.

FIGURE 3.3

The Movie Tasks pane.

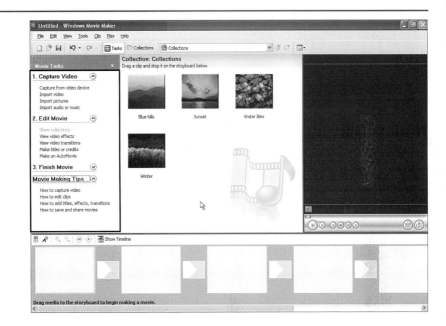

FIGURE 3.4

The Collections pane.

Want to make your movie look like an old movie? Or speed it up or slow it down? Movie Maker's video effects let you do all these things.

You can browse the video effects options by clicking View Video Effects under Edit Movie in the Movie Tasks pane.

See an effect you want? You just drag it over the clip you want to change in the Storyboard view and release it. You can preview it in the monitor by clicking Play.

If you want to perform a simple fade between two clips, you can also change to the Timeline view and then simply drag one clip onto another (see Figure 3.5). A blue line appears, showing the length of the effect.

FIGURE 3.5
Adding a fade in the Timeline view.

For a sophisticated touch, try using the fade in and fade out (to white) effects at the beginning or end of your video.

To make a film look aged, you can choose from the Old, Older, and Oldest video effects choices.

You can apply more than one effect to a clip.

To remove an effect, you right-click the effects and select Video Effects (see Figure 3.9).

You then get the dialog box shown in Figure 3.10, where you can remove (or add) an effect.

continues on page 38

You can also access video effects and transitions from the Movie Tasks pane, under Edit Movie. Again, using the menu to view your collections is simpler and easier than opening the Collections pane.

You can click Video Effects to see the effects that come with Movie Maker (see Figure 3.6). Effects are useful but not essential, and many editors don't use any effects other than fade in at the beginning of a video or fade out at the end of a video. Effects are fun to play with when you have time to explore them, but you should use them sparingly in your movies.

You can click Video Transitions to see the transitions that come with Movie Maker (see Figure 3.7). Although there are lots of transitions, 99% of the time, you only need to use one transition: the dissolve. (You'll learn more about dissolves later in this chapter.) Again, you can play around with transitions and explore them when you have time.

The Video Monitor

On the right side of the screen is the video monitor, where you can preview video clips and edits before saving them.

NOTE
You can make the video monitor bigger or smaller. To do so, you just position your cursor over the left edge of the monitor and then click and drag the edge to resize the monitor window.

The Storyboard View

At the bottom of the Movie Maker screen is a horizontal row that looks like a filmstrip (see Figure 3.8). This is called the Storyboard view,

FIGURE 3.6

Movie Maker video effects.

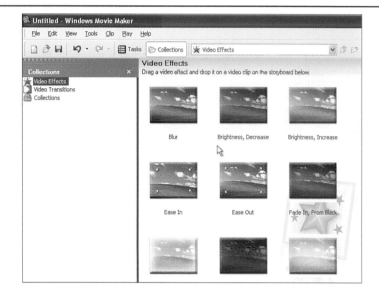

FIGURE 3.7

Movie Maker video transitions.

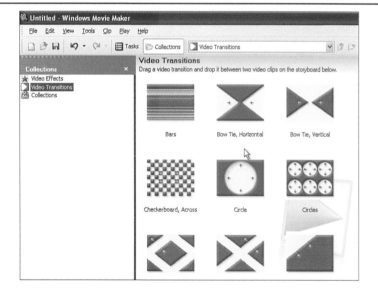

FIGURE 3.8

The Storyboard view.

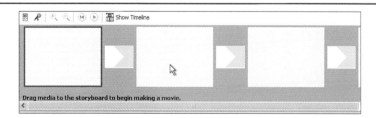

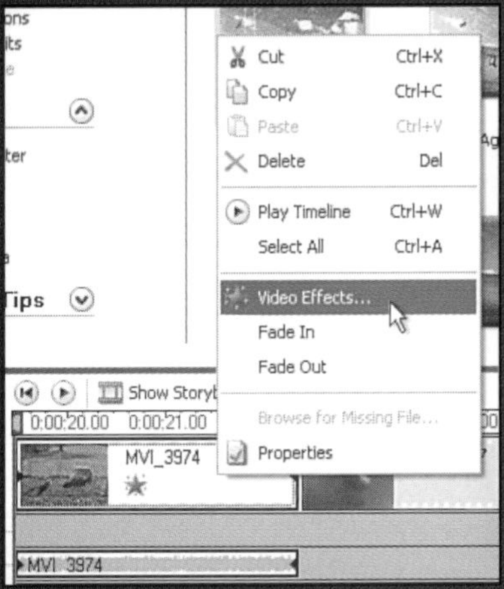

FIGURE 3.9
Accessing video effects.

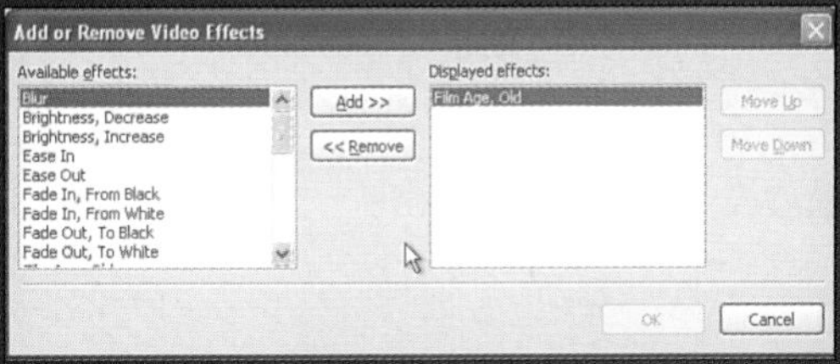

FIGURE 3.10
Adding and deleting multiple video effects.

If you want an effect on only part of a clip, you split the clip to create a separate clip in the Storyboard or Timeline view that is the one you want to apply the effect to.

To learn more about making fast- or slow-motion clips, see the sidebar "Using Video Effects to Slow Up, Slow Down, or Flip Shots" in Chapter 7, "Project 3: Making Sporting Event Movies."

and it's the editor's workhorse. You'll be using this area to edit your video. It shows the clips you put into your movie, in the order in which you arrange them.

The Timeline View

If you want to see a Timeline view of your video, you can click the button labeled Show Timeline. Movie Maker then replaces the Storyboard view with the Timeline view (see Figure 3.11).

The Storyboard View Versus the Timeline View

The Storyboard and Timeline views give you different views of your video.

Whereas the Storyboard view shows you a frame from the beginning of each of your clips (plus video transitions), the Timeline view shows you more about other elements, including the video frames, audio, music, and titles.

Let's look at a sample movie project from both the Storyboard and Timeline views. The simplified view in the Storyboard view, as shown in Figure 3.12, emphasizes the visual building blocks of the movie. The more complex Timeline view, as shown in Figure 3.13, shows you all the elements. Both have their virtues and uses.

Movie Maker Projects

A video is called a *project* in Movie Maker. Projects are the code that knits together all the various pieces of a video, including video, audio, music, pictures, transitions, effects, and more. Project filenames end with **.MSWMM**.

FIGURE 3.11

The Timeline view.

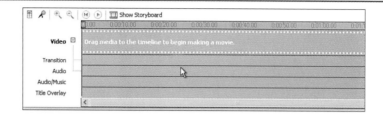

FIGURE 3.12

Like a filmstrip, the Storyboard view displays the visual elements of a movie.

FIGURE 3.13

Compared to the Storyboard view, the Timeline view provides more of an overall project overview, displaying more information about the audio elements and compressing the visual display.

Projects are not the actual video, audio, photo, or other files. If you move your video, audio, or photo files from one location to another, you have to edit your project to let Movie Maker know the new location of your files. Your Movie Maker project is, in a way, an *index* of how all the elements of your video relate to each other. Another way to think of this is that the Movie Maker file is the *connective tissue* that ties all your movie elements together. This is why Movie Maker needs you to keep all your files in the original locations you gave them; if you move files, Movie Maker tells you it can't find them (until you provide the new location information).

In this overview tour, you've seen the various components of Movie Maker and how much you can do with its simple, easy-to-use interface. Movie Maker puts all you need to edit video at your fingertips.

Your First Editing Exercise

Now that you've gotten the lay of the Movie Maker land, it's time to dive in: It's time to get started using Movie Maker to edit your first video!

For a first project, you should edit a few shots together so you can see how the process works and get a feel for how Movie Maker works. It's a good idea to do a few, practice edits just to learn how to use the program, without having any pressure to finish a project while you are learning how the process works.

After you learn how to import video and follow the basic editing steps in Movie Maker, you can make a real video project. The following sections walk you through these steps:

1. Check disk space.
2. Connect your camcorder to your computer.
3. Capture video.
4. Import music.
5. Import photo.
6. Organize and combine your collections.
7. Edit.
8. Trim clips.
9. Add music.
10. Add transitions.
11. Add titles.
12. Rough cut to fine cut.
13. Finish video.

Step 1: Check Disk Space

Do you have enough disk space to edit? In addition to the 2GB of hard disk space you need to install and run Movie Maker, you need to have more space available for putting video onto your computer's hard drive or on an external hard drive.

External hard drives are a good investment if you'll be making movies that are longer than a few minutes. To edit an hour-long program, you need at least 25GB of space. Of that, 13GB is for video files, and Movie Maker needs 12GB more of temporary space for processing the video files during editing. You also need extra hard disk space if you plan to create DVDs.

If you are using an external hard drive for your video files, you need to be sure to connect it to your computer before you begin. And if you will be importing video onto an external hard drive, you still need to connect your camcorder to your computer. Then you need to save your video files onto your hard drive.

NOTE

Don't try to connect your camcorder directly to your external hard drive, even if that's where you want to store your video files. You need to tell Movie Maker to put the video there after you launch Movie Maker's Video Capture Wizard.

Step 2: Connect Your Camcorder to Your Computer

Next, you need to get out the FireWire (also called IEEE 1394) cable that connects your computer and your camcorder. You'll see that the FireWire camcorder-to-computer cable has two different ends—a small one with pins that goes into your camcorder and a larger fitting that connects to the FireWire port on your computer. You need to connect both ends of the cable. In Figure 3.14, the cable end with the pins is on top; this is the one that goes into your camcorder. The cable end on the bottom connects to the FireWire port on your computer.

Next, you need to turn on your camcorder and select the VCR (not camera) or Playback mode, as shown in Figure 3.15.

You can control the rewind, play, and fast-forward modes on your camcorder from Movie Maker, so you don't need to use the camera controls when you're ready to view video in Movie Maker.

NOTE

If your computer does not have a digital video capture card (a requirement covered in Chapter 1), you won't be able to import video. If there is no FireWire port on your computer, this may indicate that you do not have a video capture card. You may be able to purchase a card that is compatible with your computer and install it.

FIGURE 3.14

The FireWire cable connects your camcorder to your computer.

FIGURE 3.15

When you're ready to import video from your camcorder to your computer, you select the VCR mode for video playback.

Step 3: Capture Video

Now you're ready to capture video. (I agree: *Capture* is a funny term for describing the process of importing video. After all, you're not going to be using a lasso!) After you launch Movie Maker, you see the main Movie Maker screen you saw earlier in this chapter, with the Movie Tasks pane on the left. At this point, you need to click the arrow next to Capture Video to show the options underneath it.

Launching the Video Capture Wizard

In Movie Maker, from the Movie Tasks pane, you select the first option: Capture from Video Device. This launches the Video Capture Wizard, which helps you capture video.

The Captured Video File Screen

When you are prompted by the wizard's Captured Video File screen, type the name of your file and select the location where you want your videos to be saved (see Figure 3.16).

Filenames are important and help you stay organized throughout a project. You should use a descriptive filename; for example, **school exterior** is better than **shot23**. You can identify clips more easily when you use descriptive names.

On this screen, you also need to select the hard drive you want to save your video files to and then click Next.

Video Setting

On the next wizard screen, you need to choose the video quality setting (see Figure 3.17). The first option is Best Quality for Playback on My Computer (Recommended); select it for this exercise to keep things simple. Then click Next.

Capture Method

Next, the wizard asks you how you would like to capture your video—automatically or manually:

▶ **Capture the Entire Tape Automatically—** If you know you want to import all the video you shot, you should select this option. You should use this option only if you're sure you want everything on your tape.

▶ **Capture Parts of the Tape Manually—** Because video takes up a lot of hard drive space, it's a better practice to import only the usable portions of your video. Therefore, you should generally select this option.

For this exercise, you should select Capture Parts of the Tape Manually so you get to know how this works.

For this exercise, you should also check the box Show Preview During Capture so you can see the process, and then click Next.

The Capture Video Screen

On the wizard's Capture Video screen, you can find the beginning of a clip you want to use and then rewind the tape a few seconds before

FIGURE 3.16

The Captured Video File screen: naming your movie.

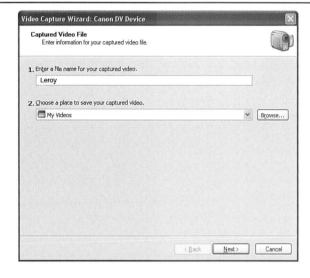

FIGURE 3.17

The Captured Video File screen: selecting the video quality.

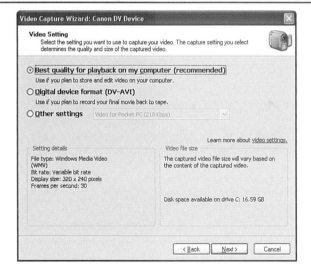

that clip starts to give yourself room to edit the clip. Then you click Start Capture. After you let the clip play, you should wait a few seconds and then click Stop Capture.

If you know the length of a clip that you want to capture, you can check the box Capture Time Limit and enter the duration of that clip.

If you have 2 minutes of video to capture, it will take your computer 2 minutes to import it.

Figure 3.18 shows an example of what the Capture Video screen looks like.

When you're finished capturing your video clip, at the bottom of the screen, click Finish.

The Import Screen

Now the Video Capture Wizard copies the temporary file to your disk. Movie Maker puts the video file into a new collection. You need to wait for the importing files process to complete.

Step 4: Import Music

If you have any music to import for this video, now is the time to add it to your collections.

From the Movie Tasks pane, you choose Import Audio or Music (under Capture Video). Then you navigate to the music file you want to use and click it. Then you select Import. Your music track appears in the Collections pane in the center of your screen (see Figure 3.19).

Step 5: Import Photo

If you want to use any digital photos in a movie, you need to add them to your collections. The process is very similar to that for adding music.

FIGURE 3.18

Capturing video.

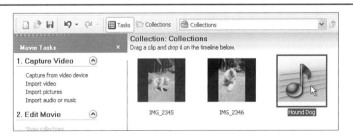

FIGURE 3.19

Importing music.

From the Movie Tasks pane, you select Import photo. Then you navigate to the photos you want to use and click them. Next, you select Import. Your photo appears in the Collections pane in the center of your screen. Movie Maker automatically creates a 5-second video clip from each photo you import (see Figure 3.20).

FIGURE 3.20
Importing photos.

Congratulations! You've imported all the elements you need—video, music, and/or photos—to create your first movie!

Step 6: Organize and Combine Your Collections

If you imported only video, all your files should be in one collection. If you have audio or photos in collections separate from your video, you need to organize them all into one collection. You should cut and paste your elements from the different collections into one collection to make editing easier.

MUSIC DOWNLOADS FOR MOVIES

Want to add some music to a movie? Many websites provide free or paid downloads you can legally use to edit into movies. You can preview the music online at all the sites listed here.

Free Sites

Freeplay Music—This website, www.freeplaymusic.com, features more than 800 free MP3 music tracks that you can legally use for free for home or school movies. (Read the site terms for using music for licensing if you have questions about licensing the music for for-profit use.)

CNET Downloads—CNET's http://music .download.com offers thousands of legal, free music downloads from independent musicians around the world.

More free tracks—Apple's iTunes Music Store, Amazon.com, and some of the other paid download music sites listed below offer free weekly music downloads. Check the sites for details. You'll also find more free, legal music online—just search the Internet for more sources.

Pay Sites

iTunes Music Store—Apple's iTunes Music Store has more than 1.5 million songs to choose from, including a limited number of free downloads that change weekly. You need to download iTunes for PC from the Apple iTunes Music Store to use this site. The iTunes Music Store sells more than 70% of the legal music downloads sold online. Visit www.apple.com/itunes.

MSN Music—Microsoft's MSN Music features more than 1 million songs for 99¢ each. Visit www.music.msn.com.

continues

Amazon.com—Amazon.com features hundreds of free and thousands of paid downloads. Visit www.amazon.com.

Walmart.com—Walmart's price is 88¢ for each track. Visit www.walmart.com.

Yahoo! Music Unlimited—Yahoo!'s Music Unlimited offers more than 1 million songs for 79¢ each. Visit www.music.yahoo.com.

Real's Rhapsody—Real's Rhapsody music service offers more than 1 million songs, with downloads priced at 79¢ each. See www.real-rhapsody.com.

Magnatune—Looking for some wonderful instrumental music for your movie? While you can find many of the latest hits on commercial music websites, it can be hard to find a great instrumental to edit into your movie. Magnatune is one of my new favorite music download sites because it offers lots of high-quality instrumental music—and at low cost. It's also a good source when you want to find something everyone hasn't heard before. It features more than 200 independent musicians and 5,000 songs; downloading an MP3 album costs $5 to $8 or more. Visit www.magnatune.com.

Step 7: Edit

Now you're ready to edit. You've been very patient so far, gathering your elements and doing all the background work. Now it's time to have some fun. You simply select and drag the video clip or photo that you want to appear at the beginning of your movie from the center of the screen in your Collections pane down to the Storyboard or Timeline view.

Figure 3.21 shows a highlighted video clip, outlined in gray.

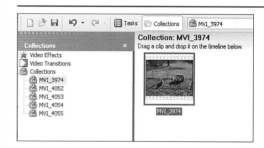

FIGURE 3.21

Video clips in a collection.

When you drag and drop the clip into the Timeline (or Storyboard) view, it drops into the beginning of the video, as shown in Figure 3.22. You can rearrange clips in the order you want—or delete them from your movie—in the Timeline view or Storyboard view.

If you decide you don't want this clip in your movie, you simply highlight the clip in the Timeline view (by clicking and holding down the mouse button) and press the Delete key. The clip is still available in the Collections pane, but it is not included in the movie.

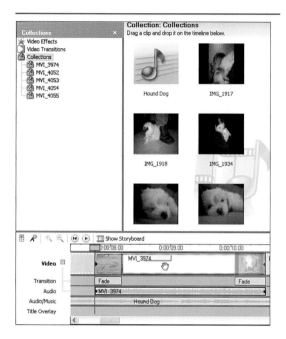

FIGURE 3.22

After you drag and drop a clip from your collection into the Timeline (or Storyboard) view at the bottom of the screen, your video clip displays.

You can continue dragging and dropping clips into the Storyboard or Timeline view to make your movie.

As you begin to accumulate more clips, you can use the scrollbar (in Figure 3.23, it's where the cursor is) at the bottom of the Storyboard or Timeline view to navigate more easily through the program.

Step 8: Trim Clips

Now that you have a number of clips in order, it's time to get out the pruning shears and trim your clips (see Figure 3.24). Is a clip too long? Click the clip, either at the beginning or the

Want to learn more about the creative art of editing? Two inspiring DVDs take you inside the world of editing, profiling editors at work and honoring their art form in television and feature films.

TV: Journeys Below the Line: 24/The Editing Process

The educational, 30-minute DVD *Journeys Below the Line: 24/The Editing Process* takes you inside the Fox series *24*. Hosted by actor Kiefer Sutherland, it features interviews with the script supervisor, the editors, and the show's postproduction supervisor, to help you understand the complex process of editing a fast-paced weekly network drama.

The DVD, part of a planned series, was created under the auspices of the Academy of Arts and Television Sciences Foundation (a nonprofit arm of the industry group that awards the Emmys), and it comes with a CD-ROM of educational extras. You can find more details about the DVD as well as download a sample page of the script, script notes, editor's log, and other production documents at the project's website, www.journeysbelowtheline.com.

Motion Pictures: The Cutting Edge: The Magic of Movie Editing

The editor's art is usually invisible, but *The Cutting Edge: The Magic of Movie Editing*, an inspired and intimate behind-the-scenes look at film editors, puts it center stage, tracing the history of editing from the start of the motion picture to today's top hits. This 99-minute feature DVD from Warner Home Video) features a star-studded cast of many of the industry's most talented editors (*Aviator* editor Thelma Schoonmaker, *Kill Bill* editor Sally

continues on page 49

end, and you are then able to drag the blue line with double red arrows to shorten it. The monitor displays the video as you move it. Then you go to the in (or beginning) point or end point that you want and release the mouse; your clip is then trimmed. It's that easy!

Again, trimming a clip in the Storyboard or Timeline view doesn't trim it in your collection. If you want to revert to the full-length clip, you can do that at any point.

Splitting a Clip

What happens when you want to take out something in the middle of a clip? The answer is to split the clip into two. You'll probably need to use this feature often.

You can split a clip anywhere you want to, by using the Split Clip button at the bottom right of the screen. You position the video where you want to split it and then click the Split Clip button, as shown in Figure 3.25.

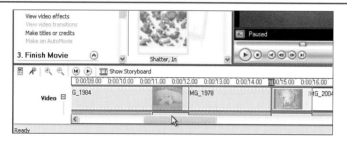

FIGURE 3.23

Assembling clips in the Timeline view.

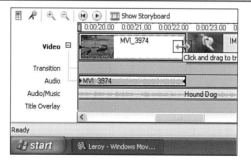

FIGURE 3.24

Trimming a clip.

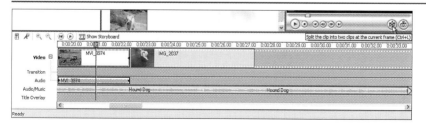

FIGURE 3.25

Splitting a video clip using the Split Clip icon. In this screen, you see the cursor arrow (way over on the right, just above the Timeline) on the Split Clip icon.

Step 9: Add Music

Adding music makes a movie much more lively. It's fun to sample and choose the music to go with your clips. You should listen to enough selections to make sure you get the right fit between your images and the emotions in the music. It may take some time. Experimenting with different musical choices is a great exercise in learning just how powerful music can be.

When you add music, you can choose to mute the original audio on your video file or mix it together with the music you add. You have the flexibility to choose to use any of these options throughout your movie: You can use both music and your original audio at times, and you can have just music or just your original audio in portions of your movie.

Once you've imported your music, you can click Show Collections under Edit Movie in the Movie Tasks pane. Then you highlight your music in the Collections pane and drag and drop it into the Timeline view in the audio/music track at the point where you want it to play. Then you release it.

If you're using music in your movie, you need to consider whether the video and audio will end at the same point. If your music is only 1 minute long and your video is 3 minutes long, you need to either loop the music over and over or trim the video to 1 minute in length.

If you prefer to use a sound effect rather than music, you can also do this in Movie Maker. You import a sound effect the same way you import music, adding it to your collection.

Because Movie Maker has only two audio tracks, you can only use music or a sound

Menke, and *War of the Worlds* editor Michael Kahn, to name a few), as well as interviews with directors including Quentin Tarantino, George Lucas, and Steven Spielberg.

The film also covers editor Walter Murch during the making of the film *Cold Mountain*, taking you inside the editing room as Murch edits the film, using pioneering digital video editing technology.

For an inside interview with producer Alan Heim about the making of *The Cutting Edge*, see www.editorsguild.com/newsletter/ NovDec04/novdec04_alan_heim.html.

SOUND EFFECTS DOWNLOADS FOR MOVIES

You'll be surprised at how much adding sound effects can add depth and drama to a movie. You may have never thought about it before, but the perfect "cha-ching" can liven up a movie. Sound effects are not just about thunder and lightning. Did you know there are sound effects for wizard spells, too?

Movie Maker comes with a small library of sound effects, but you might want to get more. Lots of great websites offer free or paid downloads you can legally edit into your movies. You can preview the sound effects online at all of the sites listed here.

Warning: Be prepared to be intrigued when you start sampling sound effects. You may find that you start thinking of ways to use sound effects that you've never imagined before!

Free Sites

Microsoft—Microsoft offers a free Windows Movie Maker Creativity Kit (in the Windows Media Bonus Pack for Windows XP) with free sound effects from Sounddogs.com, a major Hollywood movie sound effects provider. You can download the Bonus Pack free from www.microsoft.com/windows/windowsmedia/download/bonuspack.aspx.

continues on page 52

effect, but not both, if you have audio in a video track.

Adjusting Audio Levels

You can right-click an audio file in the Timeline view and choose Volume to get the Audio Clip Volume dialog box, where you can change the audio level of music or the audio in your video (see Figure 3.26).

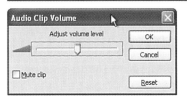

FIGURE 3.26
Adjusting audio clip volume.

Mixing Audio Levels

Movie Maker has a very cool way to let you vary the audio levels of your video sound and music tracks: You can use the Set Audio button, which is located on the left side of the screen (the cursor is over it in Figure 3.27).

Clicking the Set Audio button opens the Audio Levels dialog box, which allows you to turn up or tone down the music relative to the audio from the video (and vice versa). Moving the slider left and right varies the audio coming from these two sources. Closing this box saves your setting.

Step 10: Add Transitions

To add a transition to your video, from the Movie Tasks pane, you select View Video Transitions and drag and drop the transition over your video in the Timeline or Storyboard view. Then you can preview transitions in the video monitor.

In most cases, you should use the Dissolve transition. This is a gentle, gradual way of going from shot to shot. If you want to call attention to a transition, however, you can use a flashier transition. It's often good to use the same transition repeatedly in a movie to get a visual rhythm going. Or you can just go wild and use every transition in Movie Maker. (Kids love to do silly stuff like this.)

Step 11: Add Titles

To add titles to your movie, from the Movie Tasks pane, you select Make Titles or Credits under the Edit Movie category. Then you decide, in the screen that appears next, where in your movie you would like the titles to appear (see Figure 3.28).

Next, you are prompted to enter your text. You can preview the title in the video monitor. You can click Change the Title Animation or Change the Text Font and Color to see other choices. There are many options to choose from, and each one adds a different character and personality to your video, so take the time to find the title animation, font, and color you like best.

When you're satisfied with your title selection, you can click Done, Add Title to Movie.

FIGURE 3.27

Mixing sound levels by using the Set Audio button's Audio Levels dialog box.

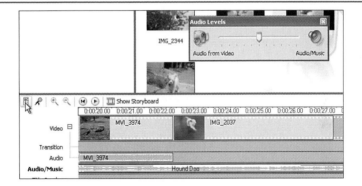

FIGURE 3.28

Adding a title to your movie.

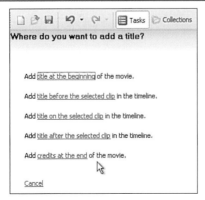

Partners in Rhyme—You'll find dozens of free public domain sound effects here. This site also sells sound effects. Visit www.partners inrhyme.com (see Figure 3.29).

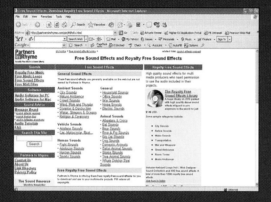

FIGURE 3.29
The Partners in Rhyme website.

Pay Sites

Sounddogs.com—If you can't find what you're looking for at Sounddogs.com, you're in trouble! This go-to site is the largest sound effects library online, with more than 47,000 sound effects available. You can have hours of fun just previewing the various effects. Prices vary widely from $1 and up, depending on the length and format of the sound effect you choose. "Dog packs" that feature a number of sounds are also available. Sounddogs.com also features paid music downloads. Visit www.sounddogs.com.

Step 12: Rough Cut to Fine Cut

What are a rough cut and a fine cut? These filmmaking terms help define the stage of a project:

▶ **Rough cut**—A *rough cut* is a basic edit, with the clips in a logical order, the music and audio in place, and the titles and credits inserted. You can think of it as a first draft.

You look at a rough cut of your movie to make sure things make sense and that the basic structure is working. At this stage, you may want to reorder a sequence or delete some footage that isn't working or is making your movie drag.

▶ **Fine cut**—A *fine cut* is an edited version that is pretty close to finished, in which all the clips have been trimmed, the audio and levels are mixed for optimal playback, and the titles and credit are inserted. You can think of it as a nearly final draft.

At the fine cut point, you're close to finishing, and you just want to check to make sure things look good. You can evaluate what minor adjustments might need to be made and do the final tweaking to make your movie a masterpiece!

When going from the rough cut to the fine cut, you need to watch your video and see how it looks. Is the audio where you want it? Are the shots in the right order? Do you like the transitions and effects you've used? You probably have a bit of editing to do, so take care of business: Trim video clips if you need to, adjust the music, and fix any other details to improve your video.

You should spend time trimming clips and tightening things up. It can really transform your video. This is what editing's all about!

NOTE

Don't skimp on this phase. You've come this far, and perfection is within your reach, so make your video what you really want it to be. The finishing touches make all the difference between an amateur effort and a video that will make you feel proud.

Step 13: Finish Video

When everything in your video is just the way you want it, you're ready to save it. You'll learn all about this in Chapter 4.

Let Your Computer Do the Editing: Using AutoMovie

Too lazy to spend time editing your clips and just want to make a quick little highlights video (for instance, to email to someone)? Or do you just want to make or share something quickly before you sit down and really edit all your clips at length? Using AutoMovie is a quick and easy (though limited) way to make movies in a snap.

AutoMovie selects brief snippets of a movie—especially medium or close-up shots, or action shots— and edits them together. In almost all cases, the audio you recorded with your movie won't make sense in the AutoMovie version, so you should use music!

Here are the basic steps in using AutoMovie:

1. **Create or select a collection.** You need to create a collection of the video clips you want to use. (You need a minimum of 30 seconds of video and music.) If you are using photos in your movie, Movie Maker

USING TITLES TO TELL A STORY

Titles can do much more than be the opening name at the beginning of a movie or the credits at the end. You can use titles to add drama, humor, or context to a movie. The following are some ways you can use titles:

▶ "Chapterize" your movies with titles—You can use titles as interludes between segments of video, creating chapters in a program. This is especially helpful when you're connecting clips that don't have a natural relationship to one another.

▶ Give the audience breathing room—For longer movies, using titles in between sections gives your audience a moment to breathe or transition from one subject to the next.

▶ Add audio to titles—Using a short snippet of music repeatedly over each chapter frame is a nice touch that can tie your whole movie together.

▶ Break up the rhythm—Titles can break up the rhythm if you have a few angles in a video or if the speed of the video is monotonous. Too much of anything can be a bad thing; you can use titles to break up movies into smaller chunks that become much more lively through the interaction of different rhythms. Titles can add a more interactive dynamic.

▶ Use choice phrases—It's important to make sure a title sets the stage for the segment by using just the right words. Sometimes you need to say the obvious, and other times you need to say something more indirect. You can experiment with different titles and see what effect each one has.

continues

You'll be surprised at how powerful titles can be when they're used well in your movie.

▸ **Headline what's coming up**—You can use a memorable quote in a title or you can headline a fun or notable audio phrase to play in a movie. This reinforces the phrase when the audience hears and sees it in the movie.

▸ **Use titles to pose questions**—Is someone in your movie saying something that the audience will have no context for when they hear the statement? Or did you have to cut out the question in your movie because you yourself asked it off-camera? If so, you can insert a title that poses a question (and the subject could be answering that question). You'll be surprised at how often this works in focusing on a topic in a movie.

puts them onscreen for 6 seconds each (so you need at least five photos to make a photos-only AutoMovie).

You can add just the video and/or photos you want, or you can let AutoMovie choose from all the elements in your collection. To select the elements you want, you drag and drop them into the Storyboard or Timeline view at the bottom of the screen.

2. **Add music.** You need to add the music you want (a minimum of 30 seconds) to this collection. Alternately, you can add the music from within AutoMovie.

3. **Open AutoMovie.** From the Movie Tasks pane, under Edit Movie, click Make an AutoMovie (see Figure 3.30).

FIGURE 3.30

Selecting Make an AutoMovie.

4. **Choose an AutoMovie style.** As shown in Figure 3.31, you need to select an AutoMovie editing style. AutoMovie gives you five choices:

FIGURE 3.31

Selecting an AutoMovie style.

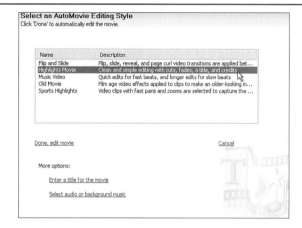

- ▸ Flip and Slide gives you flashy transitions.
- ▸ Highlights Movie makes a movie using basic transitions and titles.
- ▸ Music Video cuts your video to the beat of the music.
- ▸ Old Movie puts vintage film effects on your movie.
- ▸ Sports Highlights applies fast pans and zooms to your movie.

If one AutoMovie style doesn't include all the titling, transitions, or effects you want, you can add those by editing your AutoMovie after AutoMovie has worked its magic, by using the regular Movie Maker features. If you're undecided, you should just try Highlights Movie. Or you can experiment; you can make a variety of AutoMovies of the same collection to see what AutoMovie does with the footage in different AutoMovie styles.

5. **Enter a title and music.** Under More Options, you enter a title and add the music. (If you already have music in your collection, AutoMovie uses that music.)

Left to its own devices, AutoMovie uses the name of your first clip if you don't type in your own title, so you should enter what you want to see on this screen. When you click Done, Edit Movie, AutoMovie displays your new movie in the Timeline view.

6. **Edit your AutoMovie (optional).** Note that if you sort of like your AutoMovie but want to edit it more, you can.

Look at the AutoMovie in the Timeline view to see whether the title and credits are correct. You can change the title animation, font, or color on this screen, or you can rearrange the order of the clips. You can double-click any visual (including a title or credit) to make changes. Then you can preview the AutoMovie.

7. **Save your AutoMovie.** If you like your AutoMovie, you can save it as a project (by choosing File, Save Project). Then you can save it as a movie file by choosing File, Save Movie File. In the Save Movie Wizard, you select Save to Playback on My Computer. (See Chapter 4 for more options.)

Top 10 Tips for Editing Video

Now that you've learned the mechanics of using MovieMaker, it's time to focus on the *creative* aspects of editing. This top 10 tips list will help you learn about structuring your movie.

1. Create a Beginning, a Middle, and an End

A movie can be as simple as a slideshow set to music or as complex as a story. In any case, you need to create a movie that has a beginning, a middle, and an end, so you need to think about how to set the scene, have things happen early in your movie, sustain the action, and then create a rousing finale or find a natural ending.

Sometimes you'll want to use your clips in the order in which you shot them. Other times, you'll want to rearrange clips. You should play with various scenarios and preview them in the monitor. You'll begin to see what works.

You might be overwhelmed with too many choices. Don't get bogged down trying to find the perfect order—just do the best you can!

2. Select the Clips You Like Best

Go for the emotion. Look for moments where there's spontaneity or life! Great moments make great movies people will enjoy watching. You can import all your best bits, even if you don't yet know how they will all fit together.

Is the lighting at a certain point so dark that the scene doesn't maintain interest? Or is something so interesting happening that the lighting doesn't really matter? Is the audio audible and loud enough? Or was the microphone not able to pick up the sound? Don't be afraid to edit out anything that can't be heard well.

You should import all your favorite moments so you'll have the building blocks you need to make a great movie.

3. Make Sequences

Chapter 2, "Shooting Digital Movies," covers shooting sequences, using a mixture of long, medium, and close-up shots. If you shot a variety of shots, you can use 5 to 10 seconds of each one to create sequences.

When you get the hang of making sequences, you'll be able to edit more easily. Think of sequences as sentences or paragraphs that provide a linear flow. You need to make sure each sequence moves your video along.

Sequences also prevent you from feeling overwhelmed. Remember: Words make sentences, sentences make paragraphs, and so on. You should make a sequence here and a sequence there, and build your movie step by step.

4. Less Is More

Don't be afraid to cut, cut, cut. Learn the virtues of ruthlessness when it comes to editing. Remember that less is often more. Putting in only the best shots will make your movie more fun to watch.

In documentary filmmaking, in general, filmmakers expect to shoot at least 10 times more than they use in the final film. That means that 90% of what they shoot ends up on the editing room floor. Only the best 10% or less of their footage is in the finished movie. The secret to success is putting in only the shots that work best—and having the courage to cut what doesn't work. Here are some tips for keeping only the best shots:

▶ **Use 5 to 15 seconds per shot**—You should edit your shots to last 5 to 15 seconds per shot, as a general rule of thumb, unless there is some action that lasts longer and is compelling to watch. You can use shots that are less than 5 seconds, too; but you should try to maintain a rhythm. For example, if you use a lot of 10-second shots and only one 2-second shot, you should make sure the 2-second shot isn't jarringly out of place.

▶ **Think like a sculptor**—You should expect to cut more later, after you preview your movie. The editing process is iterative; over time, you see the places where your movie may be dragging a bit. Split clips, trim clips—whittle away!

5. Learn How to Edit Audio

Editing audio is probably one of the biggest new skills to learn in making movies. Most of us have made photo albums or slideshows, but few of us have ever edited audio. Understanding how to use audio will make you a better movie maker.

If you're using the audio you shot with your movie, you can use it to structure your clips. The rhythms of people's language will give you in and out points. Feel free to edit out parts of people's sentences, as long as what you keep in your movie makes sense. You'll start to hear language in a new way during the editing process.

Paying attention to how audio works will help you when you shoot your next movie, too.

You'll learn how important it is to get people to say things succinctly.

You need to learn how to be a nimble audio editor; you need to cut out the beginning or ending of someone's sentence and getting right to the heart of the matter, while making sure everything still make sense.

6. Use Music

Star Wars creator George Lucas once said that 50% of the movie experience is sound, and you'll quickly discover how powerfully music (or sound effects) can affect your movie.

Using music with your video or photos brings an emotional texture to your movie that wasn't there when you shot it, giving you a powerful tool to experiment with.

Aside from the emotional texture, there's the more practical consideration of how long the music track you want to use lasts. You may want to cut your video to fit the length of the music. If the music lasts longer than the movie, you need to find a good place in the music where you can fade it out.

If you don't want to use music in a movie, you can still consider putting just a tiny bit of music under your titles and/or ending credits to add a touch of emotion or a flourish.

If you're mixing music under your audio, you need to be careful to blend the audio levels well so your music doesn't drown out words you want to hear in the audio.

7. Trim Your Clips

You should make your clips last just the right amount of time in your movie. Your audience will be grateful if you don't make them watch anything boring or dull. Trimming 5 seconds here and 5 seconds there to tighten up your clips makes your movie more fun to watch in the end. It's surprising what a big impact trimming clips has on improving the quality of a movie.

Don't be shy about trimming or deleting clips—this is digital video! If you change your mind, you can always put the whole clip or any piece of it back in. That's one of the great things about movie editing!

8. Refine and Tweak Until the Last Minute

After you've made your edits and added music, titles, and/or closing credits, you should review your program and see whether there's anything that should be changed. Going from a rough cut to a fine cut is the heart of the editing process, so don't shortchange yourself (or your audience) at this stage of the game. If you're tired, take a break and come back to your project when you are fresher and more alert.

9. Get a Second Opinion

It's a good idea to have someone else look at your movie, to give you important feedback about what's working and what's not. Plus, it's fun to get some instant gratification from the parts your audience likes!

Of course, you don't have to take the advice you get about changes, but it's good to get a read on whether your movie makes sense or affected or inspired the viewer in the ways you intended.

Seeing your movie through the eyes of a viewer will help you discover things you probably didn't notice while you were editing it.

10. Finalize Your Movie

If you've gotten feedback about your movie from your audience, you can make changes. You should consider the feedback you've gotten and decide whether there are ways you want to change your movie to make it clearer or have more impact.

Summary

As you've learned in this chapter, the process of editing can be as easy or complex as you want it to be. By using your computer and basic editing software, you can make movies very easily—by using Movie Maker's AutoMovie—or you can get as complex as you want—by using the full range of editing techniques. Editing software and skills are powerful tools that you can learn to use creatively. This chapter is just the beginning of your adventures in editing.

Although editing may initially seem challenging, you will find that it gets easier over time. As you master the mechanics of using Movie Maker (or the editing software of your choice), you can spend more time developing your creative skills. You should give yourself time to grow and develop, and you should be sure to experiment and play. Enjoy the learning process: Editing, and even just learning to edit, can be a lot of fun.

For now, congratulate yourself on your initial successes. After all, you deserve it! It's quite an accomplishment to learn this material. May it be the start of something big!

CHAPTER 4

Saving and Sharing Digital Movies

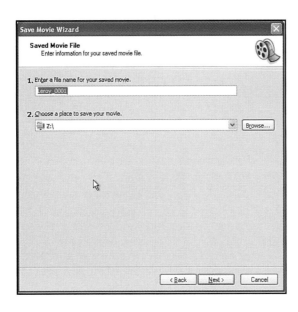

Many people consider the DVD version of a movie to be the real deal. And no wonder: DVDs let you do much more with the video you create. You can create chapters, add audio-only chapters, include photo slideshows, and—best of all—introduce your movie with beautiful, dynamic DVD menus. These DVD menus often have music and motion menu graphics that wow your audience. You can even feature clips of moving video in your DVD menus—and do they ever look great!

If you want to showcase a movie masterpiece, you need a DVD burner and DVD-authoring software.

Microsoft Partner: Sonic

Microsoft's website features a link to Sonic's MyDVD Studio, one of the most popular DVD-creation programs. You can read more about MyDVD on Microsoft's website at www.microsoft.com/windowsxp/using/moviemaker/learnmore/dvdburn.mspx.

In addition, Sonic recently purchased Roxio, another leading DVD software company, and it now sells Roxio's Easy Media Creator, another award-winning product. Both are available for purchase and download at www.sonic.com.

Free Trials of Editing/DVD-Creation Software

You can get free trial downloads of many full-featured consumer editing software programs that include DVD-burning functionality. (Sonic does not currently offer a free trial.) During the free trial, you can make DVDs to see how you like the software and then purchase your favorite program. Check out these sites for demos and details:

You've shot and edited your movie. Now it's time to save and share it. You need to get it in front of your audience, where its real life begins! This chapter covers the most common formats for saving and sharing movies—for PC playback, email, and the Web—in Movie Maker. It also provides information on how to make DVDs. (If you are using editing software other than Movie Maker, you can either skip this chapter or read it for background.)

Saving a movie can take lots of disk space, so you need to think about how you want to use the space you have. If you want to email your movie, the file size may need to be small, but if it's for playback on your computer, it could be quite large.

NOTE

If your hard disk space is limited, you can save a movie to a CD or a tape on your miniDV camcorder to use the least amount of space on your computer's hard drive.

Using Different Formats

When it comes to saving and sharing your movies, you have a lot of options. Digital video gives you the opportunity to make one file of your movie—or several. You have a lot of flexibility in deciding what format is best for your audience—or you can choose multiple formats. You can also choose to make a different *version* for each format you choose. For instance, you could make a 2-minute movie to share on the Web and a 30-minute version to play on a CD or DVD. It's quite common to make two or more files of a movie for sharing in different ways.

NOTE

If you save the same two-minute movie in multiple formats—for instance, an email version and a higher-quality version to play on your computer—remember that each file requires disk space. (They are not the same file.)

Many people want to save movies to DVD. With Movie Maker, you can't burn movies to a DVD, but it you can burn them to a CD (if you have a CD burner). Most recordable CDs are 650MB in size, so if you want to put your movie on a single CD, you'll need to make it no more than 650MB.

To make a DVD, you need additional software, which you can download for a 30-day free trial from several editing software makers' websites. (Chapter 10, "Resources for Learning," provides details.)

TIP

Remember that using a DVD is not the only way to see your movie masterpiece on TV. You can share a movie by making a miniDV tape and connecting your camcorder to your TV. (This method saves a lot of room on your hard drive.) Of course, if you want those cool DVD menus, DVD is the way to go.

Using Movie Maker's Finish Movie Section

You need to decide how you want to save and share your movie, so let's get started in the Tasks pane's Finish Movie section in Movie Maker.

- ▶ Adobe Premiere Elements— www.adobe.com/products/premiereel/ main.html
- ▶ Pinnacle Studio Plus 9— www.pinnaclesys.com/howto/ default_US.asp?langue_id=7
- ▶ Ulead MovieFactory— www.ulead.com/dmf/trial.htm
- ▶ Vegas Movie Studio+DVD— www.sonymediasoftware.com/ download/Step2.asp?DID=531

When you choose a format, Finish Movie launches the Save Movie Wizard and presents you with easy options—as well as more detailed settings, if you want a specific format—to save your movie.

With Finish Movie, you can save your movie for playback on a computer or a CD. You'll probably want to save your movie to your computer first. In addition, it's a good idea to make a backup copy on a CD or a miniDV tape.

With Finish Movie, you can also format a movie to send to others via email, the Web, or a miniDV tape (using your miniDV camcorder).

An email movie is a smaller file that you send via email. A Web-formatted movie is also (typically) smaller than the version you save to your computer.

Let's try a movie editing exercise, using the clips you edited together in Chapter 3, "Editing Basics: Movie Maker and More." In this practice exercise, you should use the Finish Movie option Save to My Computer, which allows you to save your movie to either your computer's internal drive or an external hard drive. (If you don't see any options under Finish Movie, click the arrow next to Finish Movie to see the different sections under Finish Movie.)

You should use the Save to My Computer option if you plan to make a DVD later (see Figure 4.1).

Using the Save Movie Wizard

Selecting Save to My Computer (or any of the other options under Finish Movie) launches the Save Movie Wizard, as shown in Figure 4.2.

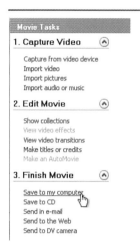

FIGURE 4.1

Saving a movie to your computer using the Tasks pane.

(This wizard is quite similar to the Capture Video Wizard you used in Chapter 3.)

You need to enter a name for your movie and tell the Save Movie Wizard where to save it.

Saving Formats and Versions

You can choose to save multiple formats and versions of a movie:

▸ **Formats**—You can save the same movie in different formats (if you want to both make a DVD of it and also email it, for instance). If you have a 3-minute movie, you can make a movie to play back on your computer. It's best to make *another* movie file for emailing by using Send in E-mail if you want to share your movie with a friend because an email file (which you can create by using Movie Maker's Save Movie Wizard) will be much smaller.

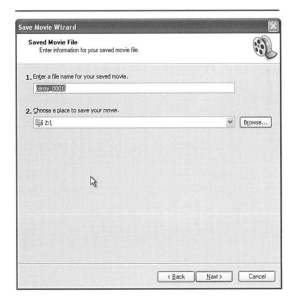

FIGURE 4.2

Naming and saving a movie by using the Save Movie Wizard.

It's a good idea to name your different files clearly; for example, for a movie called My Movie, you should name your files **MyMovieforDVD** and **MyMovieforemail**, so you can easily keep track of the different formats of the saved movies. You can probably tell which is which from the file sizes, too, but it's easier if you label them from the beginning.

▶ **Versions**—You might want to make long and short versions of a movie if you're planning to share the movie in multiple ways. After you've collected all the elements, you can leverage your efforts to make movies for different audiences and settings. It's usually (though not always) much easier and quicker to make a second, short version of your movie after you've made a long version.

Let's say you have a 20-minute movie you want to put on a DVD, and you also want to send someone a movie email of the movie. Email and Web movies are better if they are short because video files sizes are large. But large file sizes are only part of the problem. The other issue is attention span. Because it's much more compelling to watch your movie on a big screen, people may watch a 20-minute movie on a computer or DVD player, but if the movie is a postage-stamp-size Web movie, 20 minutes is often too long for the audience to maintain interest. In that case, it's a good idea to make a short version of your movie, say 2 minutes (or less), with just the highlights or best parts of your movie.

First, you save the longer version, using Save to My Computer. You can then re-edit your project and save a shorter version, using Send to e-mail (or another appropriate format).

Again, it's a good idea to name your different files clearly—for example, **MyMovieLong** and **MyMovieShort**—so you can easily keep track of the different versions of your saved movies.

Selecting Movie Settings

The Movie Settings screen gives you one option: Best Quality for Playback on My Computer (Recommended). You should select this option, which saves your movie as a .WMV file.

Determining File Size

You can look at the text at the bottom-right of the screen to see the file size. Movie Maker also tells you how much space you have available on the hard drive you selected, so you can determine whether you have room to save your movie.

Reducing File Sizes

If you don't have enough space, you can use Show More Choices to tell Movie Maker a specific file size to save your movie to. However, if you make your movie file size smaller, the movie quality is reduced. It's best not to specify a drastic reduction in file size. (However, if you want, for instance, to fit your movie on a 650MB CD, this feature is very helpful because you could enter the desired file size here and have Movie Maker calculate the settings to make the file size you want.)

Specifying Other Settings

You can save a file to dozens of different formats by using the Show More Choices option and scrolling through the pop-up menu, which has a long list of movie formats. You can even save your movie to put on a PocketPC.

For this exercise, you should use the setting Best Quality for Playback on My Computer (Recommended).

Saving a Movie

The final step in the process is for Movie Maker to save your movie, which takes awhile, depending on the length and size of the movie file.

Completing the Save Movie Wizard

When your movie is saved, you have a chance to play the saved movie. You should check the check box if you need to see the saved movie or uncheck it if you don't want to watch it now. Then you click Finish.

Creating Additional Formats and Versions

At this point, you should save any additional formats if you want to play back your movie in other environments—for instance, in email.

You could also start on a new (shorter?) version of your movie at this point. You can come back to do this another time, or you can return to the project now and edit it further, repeating these steps to save to a different format or edit to another length.

Saving to CD

Making a CD of your movie is a very good idea. You need an internal or external CD burner to make a CD of your movie. Making a CD accomplishes two goals:

▶ It frees up disk space on your computer or external hard drive. If you want to erase the movie file on your computer to make more disk space available, you can use a CD to store a digital version.

▶ It backs up your movies.

The best practice is to save two copies of your completed movie project to protect your valuable edited movie and all the work you've put into making it. Even if you have unlimited disk space (but who does?), digital files on computers are fragile—they can be accidentally erased by human beings or affected by a computer crash. A good practice is to save one copy on your hard drive (for easy editing later) and one copy on a CD for backup.

To save a movie to a CD, you put a blank CD in your CD burner. If you are using an external CD burner, you need to make sure the CD burner is connected to your computer. Then you follow the steps in the Save Movie Wizard to burn a copy of your movie to a CD.

Remember that most recordable CDs are 650MB, so if you are saving your movie to a CD and you plan to put it on a single CD, you need to make sure your file is no larger than 650MB.

Sending in Email

To send a movie in email, you select the option Send in e-mail under Finish Movie in the Tasks pane, to launch the Save Movie Wizard. The wizard saves a smaller movie file size, opens your email program, and attaches your movie. You fill in the address of the person you're sending to and click Send.

It's good email etiquette to send only small files, so be courteous!

Sending to the Web

To send a movie of a movie to the Web, you select the option Send to Web under Finish Movie in the Tasks pane, to launch the Save Movie Wizard.

The Save Movie Wizard asks you how you connect to the Web to determine the right size movie file to create, depending on the speed of the connection.

After the wizard saves your movie, it asks you where to put your movie online. If you have Web hosting, you enter that information on this screen.

PUTTING YOUR MOVIE ON THE WEB

When it comes to finding a home for your movie on the Web, many sites now offer free hosting for publicly accessible movies. Others provide hosting for a fee. Here are some of the options:

▶ Google Video—Google Video offers free movie uploading. Google Video prefers a different format (MPEG2 or MPEG4) than the WMV file you create by using Movie Maker, but it still hosts WMV files. Google Video allows both free and paid movie uploads. In order to upload your movie, you must own the copyright to your movie and meet Google Video policy guidelines. For details, visit https://upload.video.google.com/video_faq.html#overview2.

▶ Ourmedia—Ourmedia is a nonprofit group dedicated to personal media that provides free movie hosting in association with Archive.org, a nonprofit Internet archive. By opening a free account, you can publish your movie to the Web. For more information, visit www.ourmedia.org/help/publish-video.

▶ Neptune Mediashare—Microsoft has partnered with Neptune's Mediashare to provide movie hosting for a fee. Your movie can be password protected or openly available. Mediashare offers a free trial account to use and evaluate the service for 3 days. After that, hosting is $59 a year for 15MB, with larger storage options for a higher fee.

TIPS FOR MAKING YOUR MOVIES SEARCHABLE

Do you want search engines on the Internet to point people to your movie when you post it on the Web? If the answer is yes, new movie search engines want you!

Google (https://upload.video.google.com/video_faq.html#overview2) and Yahoo! (http://search.yahoo.com/mrss/submit) are actively seeking submissions for their new video search engines. Each of them offers an online way to submit your movie to help people find it. Google provides free movie uploads and accepts transcripts to help searchers find you. Yahoo! accepts RSS (Really Simple Syndication) feeds for movies posted on the Internet. Yahoo!'s movie RSS feeds allow people to subscribe to your movies. Check the Yahoo! Video Search website (http://video.search.yahoo.com/?&ei=UTF-8&p=) for details on how to create RSS feeds for this Yahoo! service.

Another site, Blinkx.tv, also offers movie submissions to its movie search site. For details, see www.blinkx.tv/beta/PodcastSubmit.

MSN and AOL may provide similar services in their new movie search features; check www.msn.com and www.aol.com for the latest details.

TIP

The Save Movie Wizard also offers to help you buy hosting online by opening a Mediashare account with Microsoft's partner Neptune. For complete information, visit www.neptune.com. See the sidebar "Putting Your Movie on the Web," in this chapter, for a list of free hosting sites.

Sending to a DV Camera

You can use the Send to DV Camera option when you want to do the following:

▶ Make a backup of your movie on miniDV tape

▶ Watch your movie on TV, using your camcorder to play your movie

If you're saving your movie to your miniDV camcorder, remember to put a blank tape in. If you have to use a previously recorded tape, you need to make sure the Record/Save tab is in the Record position. You want to avoid the tragic mistake of recording over any valuable footage on a previously used tape!

To watch your movie on TV, you connect your camcorder to your TV, using the proper cables. The cables to connect your camcorder to the TV probably came with your camcorder when you purchased it. (If not, they are usually readily available at an electronics store.)

Summary

In this chapter, you've learned how to save your movies to share in a variety of ways so you can distribute them to family members, friends, or a public audience.

You've learned about the many different formats in which you can share your movies—email, the Web, your computer, a CD, or a miniDV tape—and how best to save your movies by using Movie Maker. You've learned about the advantages of editing different versions of a movie for playback on different platforms as well as the importance of making backup copies of your movies.

Next, you'll learn how to shoot specific kinds of movie projects and have your audiences begging for more.

CHAPTER 5

Project 1: Creating Birthday Party and Baby Movies

In this chapter, you'll find out how to make birthday party and baby movies that people will enjoy. From start to finish, this chapter gives you focused tips and techniques to shoot and edit your movie.

For your shoot, you can review technical basics and read creative overviews, to find out how to get the best shots and record scenes you might not have thought about shooting. This chapter helps you edit your movie by providing a quick review of the basic steps, suggestions on using Movie Maker's AutoMovie, and a list of suggested music for your movie.

You'll also find links to online birthday party and baby movies that are fun to watch and demonstrate some of the tips and techniques discussed in this chapter.

Making Birthday Party Movies

Birthday party movies are a lot of fun to shoot. With children, there's lots of action and excitement. For adults, especially at a big birthday (turning 30, 40, 50, or more), it's a cause for celebration and perhaps even reflection. All this provides great opportunities for making movies that are entertaining to create and to watch.

If you can, edit and share birthday party movies quickly (not months later). Remember that if you shoot it well, editing can be a snap!

Making an AutoMovie (covered in Chapter 3, "Editing Basics: Movie Maker and More") is a good way to get a birthday party movie finished right away. When you find just the

perfect music track, you're halfway there. (See the sidebar "Finding the Perfect Music for Your Birthday Party or Baby Movie," later in this chapter, if you need music suggestions.) Reread the section "Let Your Computer Do the Editing: Using AutoMovie" in Chapter 3 if you need to refresh your memory on how to use AutoMovie.

It's important to think ahead about the shoot and organize yourself and your equipment to make sure you'll get the shots you need to make a great birthday party movie.

Getting Ready for Your Shoot

Your movie begins with the right preparation, including both the technical and creative aspects of your shoot:

▶ On the technical front, you need to review the essential equipment to bring to your shoot, as well as think about bringing extra, helpful items.

▶ On the creative front, you need to think about what shots you would ideally like to have in your finished movie. This chapter reviews what shots are most important to get and lists other shots that are "nice-to-haves."

For your shoot, you should remember to bring your camcorder, charged batteries (or a power cord), blank tape, and a tripod. An extra charged battery is good to have, too.

You might also want to bring along an external microphone to capture reminiscences from the birthday boy or girl and their friends, especially if this movie is for someone who's turning a significant age in life (20, 30, 40, 50, or more).

Making a birthday party movie means following the basic guidelines of shooting discussed in Chapter 2, "Shooting Digital Movies." You should vary your shots—get wide shots, medium shots, and close-ups. If you can, get all three of an interaction or activity so you'll have plenty of shots to edit together into sequences.

One of the trickiest parts of shooting parties is lighting. It's best to avoid backlighting your scenes. If backlighting is a problem, you can shoot more close-ups. If it's an indoor/outdoor party, you can shoot some scenes you want in better lighting situations.

As always, it's important to hold the camera steady. If you can use a tripod, do. If you can't use a tripod, brace the camera against your body to hold it steady as you shoot. You can do a lot of roving shooting, as long as your shots are steady.

TIP

Out for a birthday dinner but didn't bring your camcorder? If you have a video camera on your cell phone, catch a video snippet and email it to the birthday boy or girl.

Shooting a Birthday Party Movie

Many birthday party movies are pretty predictable: some milling around party shots, perhaps some present-opening shots, and the obligatory cake shot. Most of these shots are the same shots a picture taker would take at a birthday party.

What can a movie do that's special? Plenty. Most of all, it can help you tell the *story* of a birthday party and bring a lot more characters and life to it than a photo album.

If you think through ahead of time more of the creative opportunities for shooting different kinds of scenes and interviews, your birthday party movies can really shine.

The following sections describe some creative ideas for enlivening your birthday party movies. After you've read through these sections, you may find that you have many more ideas about how to make a birthday party movie that's creative and a great gift to the birthday boy or girl. Bring your ideas to your shoot.

Don't be afraid to show *whatever* is happening. Just shoot what's going on, and remember that later you can decide whether it will be funny or entertaining in your movie. Editing can set the proper context.

Shooting Party Preparations

Shoot some of the pre-party preparations—baking (or buying) the cake, decorating for the event, interviewing the cake baker/buyer about why he or she is baking (or buying) this kind of cake and what's in it. Cake decorating shots are also nice to have. If it's a bakery-made cake, get some shots of the inside and outside of the bakery.

Stories about family food lore are priceless. In my family, we have one chocolate cake (made with a secret ingredient—mayonnaise) without which any birthday would not be legitimate. Get shots of any special food items and an explanation about why they're special and other associations with this food. People love food, and they love movies about food, too.

Also shoot other party preparations, such as shopping for the party favors and deciding which "theme" paper plates and decorations to get. Edit this at high speed over good music, and you can have a very cute sequence in your movie—one that will be sure to surprise the birthday boy or girl.

Shooting the Making or Wrapping of Presents

Building a tree house, creating a doll house, or making other homemade gifts? Making or wrapping presents—small or large—is fun fodder for the birthday party movie, and this part of your party movie will be a surprise for the birthday boy or girl.

Shooting the Place

Shoot the interior and the exterior of the birthday party location. You'll only need a few seconds in your movie. For an exterior shot, you can shoot a few guests arriving to liven up the shot.

Capturing the Food

Shoot the food before and after the guests arrive. You could use quick cuts of the disappearing food during the movie to show the progression of the party or just use one before and one after shot. Or you can just use a nice shot of the before scene. Again, if there are any special food stories associated with the party, add them. Interview the chefs. Add anything about the birthday person's favorites that are included in the menu.

Shooting and Interviewing the Guests

If you're shooting children, they'll be playing and doing interesting things you can shoot. There will be plenty of action.

If you're shooting adults, getting some action will probably involve brief interviews. You could ask guests how long they've known the birthday boy or girl or what gift they're giving the person and why.

Also get shots without much talking if you want to edit together a highlights movie. A wave from individuals or a group is always a good shot to edit over music and makes sure you get everyone in the video. This is especially nice for significant year (30, 40, 50, or more) birthday party movies.

TIP

For a special birthday, ask distant friends and family members who can't make it to the event to send video birthday greetings you can give to the guest of honor and edit into your movie.

In a pinch, you could even capture your video greetings on a cell phone video camera (and edit them on your computer, if you want). Here's a fun example of this I found on the Web: http://fauxpress.blogspot.com/2005/05/instant-documentaries-happy-birthday.html.

Shooting Party Favors and Games

Pin the tail on the donkey? You bet. No birthday party movie would be complete without the birthday games and activities kids enjoy. Is there a pirate theme? Treasure hunt? Clowns? Capture all the action.

If there are party favors, don't be afraid to ask the whole group to get together for a group shot with them. Have them all blow their party favor whistles, wave little flags, or play with whatever hoopla trinkets are on hand. If it's a surprise party, you can shoot a few scenes like this before the birthday boy or girl arrives.

Talking to the Birthday Boy or Girl

Interact with the birthday boy or girl. What's special to them about turning this age? What presents are they hoping to get? What kind of cake do they like best? If they are shy or self-conscious about being on camera, get another person or a few people to be in the shot with them and have the other people ask the questions.

If the birthday boy or girl is an adult, ask what they're grateful for in life. What observations do they have about turning this new age? What are they celebrating most of all?

Shooting the Cake and Song

If you can, shoot "backstage" shots in the kitchen of candle-lighting and other last-minute preparation for the big cake moment.

Shooting the cake and song is the biggest moment of any birthday party, so find a good position where you can capture the action. Remember that you want to shoot both the birthday boy or girl and all the guests. Vary your shots. During the song, it's nice to pan around the room so you get footage of everyone singing together. If you're not using a tripod, remember to hold the camera steady!

Is this a *very* significant birthday (that is, 50, 60, 70 or more)? For anyone getting on in years, recording their life history is a great present—for the birthday person and for everyone who loves him or her. It's very thoughtful and rewarding to make a memory movie and screen it at the party as part of the festivities.

You can also take advantage of seeing out-of-town guests at the party, shoot a little interview with each one at the party, and make an enhanced version of your DVD later on.

For details on shooting a life history or making a photo slideshow movie of a life, read Chapter 9, "Project 5: Making Family Memory Movies."

Shooting the Presents

Everyone loves giving and getting presents. Get shots of the birthday person opening presents as well as shots of gifts being passed around the room. Shoot everything and use just a little bit in editing. If you want, you can edit this at high speed and put some music over it.

When I shot my godson's third birthday party, I joked that I should title it "It's Mine!" given the number of times he said it at the party (in response to other kids wanting to play with his brand-new toys). Coming from a three-year-old, this was a funny comment about the human condition and growing up.

> **TIP**
>
> Remember to protect and lock your tapes (turning the tab from Record to Save) and label everything from your shoot (if you have not already done so).

Editing Your Birthday Party Movie

After you shoot your video, what's next? Now it's time to have some fun with your footage. Pick out your best shots—the liveliest ones you have—and import them into your editing software.

Editing birthday party movies is often more fun than editing many other kinds of movies because the subject itself is good times. Usually, you're not worried about great audio and important content, so you can just turn up the music and edit away. Most often, the visuals can carry most of the story.

> **TIP**
>
> To see an inspiring great 40th birthday party movie that uses many of the tips outlined in this chapter, check out www.chrispirillo.com/help/20050123_happy_birthday.phtml. See how well the quick edits work and how the music ties everything together.

If you want to edit your movie to music alone, you can use Movie Maker's AutoMovie to create a quick highlights movie set to a great soundtrack.

In a birthday party movie, you can play with effects. Speeding up a small portion of the movie can be fun—especially with kids who are sort of hyperactive after the birthday cake—or slowing motion down, if they all crashed from sugar rushes. For details on using the Speed Up and Slow Down motion effects in Movie Maker, see the sidebar "Using Video Effects to Speed Up, Slow Down, or Flip Shots" in Chapter 7, "Project 3: Making Sporting Event Movies."

Also think about making several versions of your birthday party movie for different purposes—a little AutoMovie video email or Web video is nice for everyone to enjoy, followed up by a DVD copy for the birthday girl or boy.

If this is a significant birthday, you can create a whole life story DVD and later invite people to a screening of it via a highlights movie trailer in email or on the Web. Or, if you really have your act together, you can make a life story DVD in advance of the big party and screen it at the party.

Basic Editing Steps

Remember to be ruthless in editing and edit or delete any overly long shots that don't work. It's important to take the time to edit your movie so that it's fast paced and entertaining. Don't let some of the movie bog down; just whittle out footage that drags or slows the pace too much.

TIP

You can edit photos into your movie by using Movie Maker. For more information about adding motion to your photos, see the section, "Making an Advanced Slideshow Movie" in Chapter 9. It tells you how to use Microsoft's Photo Story 3 software to add pans and zooms (and other cool features) to still photos.

Here's a quick review of the editing steps outlined in Chapter 3:

1. Select the best portions of your footage and look for enough coverage to create a beginning, a middle, and an end.

2. Import the video into your computer and create and insert it in a Movie Maker collection.

3. Select the clips you like best and place them in the order in which you think they should go in the Timeline view or Storyboard view. Edit your shots into sequences.

4. Trim your clips.

5. Edit your clips together, using dissolves.

6. Add music.

7. Add titles.

8. Review your edited rough cut and evaluate it.

FINDING THE PERFECT MUSIC FOR YOUR BIRTHDAY PARTY OR BABY MOVIE

Adding great music to your birthday party and baby movies will bring more personality and life to them. Finding the perfect music for your birthday party or baby movies is easier than ever, using (legal, of course) free or low-cost music download sources on the Internet.

For birthday party and baby movies, some of the best places to find music are on CD, at FreePlay Music (www.freeplaymusic.com; which offers hundreds of MP3 tracks to download for free—legally, of course), and at the Apple iTunes Music Store (www.apple.com/itunes; which offers 99¢ downloads).

Here are some of the best songs to add a special touch to your birthday party movie:

▶ "Birthday" (The Beatles)

▶ "Happy Birthday" (Jim Harmon)

▶ "Happy Birthday Baby" (Jamie Chiello)

▶ "Circle Game" (Jim Harmon)

▶ "You've Got a Friend in Me" (Randy Newman)

▶ "Old Chunk of Coal" (Billy Joe Shaver or other artists)

▶ "Je Ne Regrette Rien" (Edith Piaf)

For baby movies, here are some of the best songs:

▶ "A Matter of Time" (Jim Harmon)

▶ "Baby" (Bobby McFerrin)

▶ "Brahms' Lullaby" (Jim Harmon)

▶ "Circle Game" (Jim Harmon)

▶ "Isn't She Lovely" (Stevie Wonder)

▶ "I Want to Be a Baby" (David Hall, from the CD *Bee Positive*), www.beepositive.bz (see Figure 5.1)

continues

FIGURE 5.1

"I Want to Be a Baby" is just one of the great kids' songs—that can become your movie soundtrack—on David Hall's CD *Bee Positive*.

For more music sources, also see the sidebar "Music Downloads for Movies" in Chapter 3 for a list of other sites that give you a wide selection of music selections.

9. Review your edited fine cut and make any final changes.
10. Save, share, and enjoy your finished movie.

After you've created a birthday party movie, share it with your audience. A movie lets everyone who came to the party relive the fun they had, and it gives people who weren't able to attend an entertaining look at what they missed. Making birthday party movies is simple, easy, and fun. Birthday party movies are a great way to remember the good times!

Making Baby Movies

There's probably no single event that inspires people to pick up a video camera than a new baby. Every baby's life is filled with unforgettable moments—from pregnancy to birth and beyond. From every goo to every gah, babies enchant and entertain us. Capture these precious moments in your baby movies!

Shooting a Baby Movie

Shooting movies of babies is fun; you can get completely entranced watching them for hours. But to make your movies interesting, you need to shoot a variety of scenes. You should also shoot sequences with wide, medium, and close-up shots, and you should interact with the people in your movies.

Lighting is also a consideration. You should try to avoid backlit shots. You should position yourself to get the best lighting situation, but of course, if the lighting isn't great, capturing the moment while it's happening is more important than having perfect lighting. Do your best.

The following sections describe some of the things you might want to shoot.

Shooting the Pregnancy

You can start a baby movie by shooting during pregnancy. Interview Mom (or yourself, if you're the mother, by setting up the tripod and putting yourself on camera) the day she discovers she's pregnant and at regular intervals during pregnancy. Trips to the doctor, profiles of Mom's changing belly (see Figure 5.2), Mom's cravings, Mom and Dad in birthing class, shopping for baby gear, getting the baby's room ready, the new mothers' group—all these add lots of human interest and activity to your movie.

FIGURE 5.2
Pregnancy can be part of your baby movie.

Interview Mom's girlfriends and other friends and family members to see how they think Mom and Dad will change as parents and what kind of family they will create. If this is not a first child, you can also interview other children in the family about what they think it will be like to have a baby sister or brother and what they're looking forward to.

Shooting the Baby Shower

Making a movie of a baby shower is a fun prelude to a baby's entrance into the world. Interview the guests about any wishes they have for the baby and family or any tips or advice. A baby shower movie is also a very nice gift to give. Review the section "Shooting a Birthday Party Movie," earlier in this chapter, for tips on how to shoot party events.

Shooting the Birth (Optional)

Some people want the birth to be part of their movie, and others do not. Consider what makes everyone comfortable. For some people, this is the most important moment in their lives and they want it recorded for posterity. Others do not want to add to the drama of the moment. Be sensitive to people's preferences and work with them to create what everyone wants.

Shooting Life with Baby

Firsts—baby's homecoming, baby's first feeding, baby's first diaper change, Mom and Dad learning how to change diapers, baptisms, grandparents' first visit—are all great scenes to have. Get close-ups of the baby's face as well as medium and wide shots of the baby and everyone else (see Figures 5.3 and 5.4).

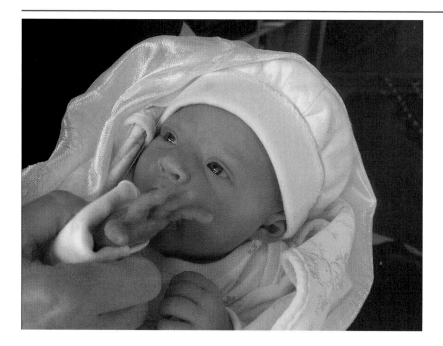

FIGURE 5.3
Every baby is a star.

TIP

Consider making an online video birth announcement. After the baby arrives, it's lovely to shoot, save, and share scenes of the family and infant from the hospital room or other birth place. If you only have photos (and no video), you can make a movie out of those still photos by using Movie Maker's import photos feature and adding music and titles. As with online baby photos, you can share this movie on the Web and send it to family members and friends.

Getting a Baby's-Eye View

After you've shot baby movie scenes (over and over and over), you might be ready to try something a but more adventurous: Try shooting a baby's-eye view of the world. What does the baby see from the crib? from the floor? from a lap? You can re-create some of these experiences.

You can put the camera in the crib and point it up at a mobile, if there is one. You can have someone bring a spoon with baby food toward the camera. Use your creativity to think of other scenes that give a first-person point of view to your movie. From these scenes alone, you can edit a hilarious movie.

Shooting Everything Baby

When a baby begins to crawl, walk, and talk, you have more exciting moments to capture. Try shooting to get a baby's-eye view of the world by putting the camera down at baby's height.

FIGURE 5.4
Welcoming the new baby is a big moment.

TIP

A good soundtrack for this kind of movie is "I Want to Be a Baby" by David Hall. I will post emails from people with their favorite best baby video music selections.

Email me if you have one to share—info@createyourowndigitalmovies.com—and I will post the entries at www.createyourowndigitalmovies.com.

TIP

"Fuller Sings" is an amusing baby video movie about a very precocious musician, and it is sure to make you smile. See it at www.crumley.org/videos/fuller_videos_2005.htm (see Figure 5.5).

FIGURE 5.5
"Fuller Sings" is a great example of creatively using titles in a baby movie.

For more online movies, enter *birthday video* or *baby movie* at your favorite search site and explore the links you find to get your creative juices flowing.

Sleeping babies can even be interesting. You can edit together a variety of shots (different angles and baby movements) to lullaby music.

You can also give a baby a prop, like a blanket or toys, to play with so you get some fun action shots to edit into your baby movie.

Shooting from Babyhood to Toddlerhood and Beyond

Keep shooting. While the first month of a baby's life is very exciting and new, shooting even just once a month over time throughout the first year and after (see Figures 5.6 and 5.7) captures the exciting growth and changes every newborn goes through. So pick up your camera from time to time and keep recording life unfolding before your very eyes.

Editing Your Baby Movie

You can review the steps in the section "Editing Your Birthday Party Movie," earlier in this chapter; everything in that section applies to editing baby movies, too.

When you edit your baby movie, keep your clips short! Babies are fascinating, but not forever!

FIGURE 5.6

A first birthday: It's time for a party—and a video!

FIGURE 5.7

Who can resist shooting such adorable stars? With talent like this, you will have lots of great material to work with.

Summary

In this chapter you've learned how to make movies that bring life to the screen, using creative approaches to shooting birthday party movies and baby movies. Using these shots lists and thinking about all the different ways to capture life will help you see how much there is to shoot. Understanding this can help you advance from shooting the way picture takers do to taking full advantage of video's enormous creative potential.

Following the steps outlined in this chapter should help you avoid some of the most common mistakes in making birthday party or baby movies:

- Dull footage (because you're shooting lots of great interactions and a variety of scenes)

- Shaky cam (because you're using a tripod or concentrating on getting good handheld shots)

- Slow-paced editing (because you're being ruthless about using only your best shots)

This chapter also provides helpful online resources—places online where you can watch birthday party and baby movies that use many of the tips and techniques outlined in this chapter. In addition, you now know where to go to find music that can add energy and a festive touch to your birthday party and baby movies.

By using these creative ideas and practical resources, you can create memorable movies people will want to watch, time and again, to relive the good times!

CHAPTER 6

Project 2: Making Travel and Vacation Movies

In this chapter, you'll learn how to make travel and vacation movies that bring home the sights, impressions, and fun of a trip. It covers technical basics and provides creative overviews that give you detailed information on how to get the best shots, capture moments you might not have considered shooting, and find online resources that can add lots of creative punch to your travel and vacation movies.

Learning how to use this information will help you make vacation and travel movies that let you relive your trip long after the suitcase is unpacked. You can make your adventures into movies that will bring back those memories.

Travel is an intrinsically interesting subject for a movie—just think of all the great on-the-road movies you've watched on the big screen. Off you go, new adventures await—and who knows what you'll see and shoot?

TIP

Want to rent some great road movies for inspiration? Try the list of road movies from the University of California at Berkeley's website at www.lib.berkeley.edu/MRC/roadmovies.html# roadmovies. My favorite is Road Scholar (available online at www.amazon.com and www.moviesunlimited.com).

Finding your travel movie style is one of the best parts of making travel movies. Shooting and editing your own travel movie puts you and your creativity in the driver's seat. You don't have to buy all the travel movies in the national park store anymore—you can make your own! You can make a personal video to enjoy long after the vacation is over.

The single biggest factor in making your travel movies a success is accessibility, so have your video camera handy. Keep your camcorder loaded with blank tape and charged batteries, so you can shoot at a moment's notice. When you're in a national park and a bear is crossing the road, you want to be able to pick up your camera and start shooting right away!

Remember, though, to protect your camera— keep it in your camera bag and don't store it in a hot car.

Creative Approaches to Making Travel and Vacation Movies

Your travel movie can be much more than just pretty pictures. Still photos of beautiful scenery can make a great slideshow, but it's hard to make a great movie of just scenery (unless you add music). Interacting with people and places will help you make a more compelling movie.

Travel movies can be full of characters. So meet locals and videotape them. Talk to and shoot a cafe owner or a lobsterman, surfers, or a lady selling tomatoes; you'll be amazed at what people tell you. (Remember that you have the power to edit out anything when you're back at your computer.) While you're in the field, connect and engage with people— and shoot away!

Ask people where the locals like to eat best— and what should you order there—and then go there. Videotape the menu, your meal, the waitress (perhaps), and your own personal standup restaurant review (using the tripod) afterward. Even just one brief sequence like this can be very funny.

Don't overlook the characters you are traveling with—including yourself. You'll probably be shooting your traveling companions on your trip, but don't forget to add one very important character in your movie: you. Ask your friends or family members to take over shooting at times.

If you can't get anyone to shoot you on camera because they don't know how to use the camcorder, set up your tripod, frame a shot large enough for you to appear in, push Record, and get in front of the camera yourself. Or get the whole gang, including you, on camera together.

You can set up your shot in front of a landmark or spectacular view and talk to the camera about what is happening and where you are. Then you can shoot what you've described (without you in the frame) to have extra footage to edit in so your audience can experience what you've been talking about.

TIP

The feature documentary *Grizzly Man* (directed by Werner Herzog) is a brilliant example of a movie made from self-filmed footage. You can rent it for inspiration.

When you edit your video, remember that you can make as many versions as you like—from a short highlights movie to a full-on epic. You can share different versions with different audiences or use a quick highlights movie online to get people to come over for a big at-home screening of the longer movie.

Think ahead about the shoot and organize yourself and your equipment to make sure you'll get the shots that it takes to make a great travel movie.

Getting Ready for Your Shoot

Your movie begins with the right preparation. Preparation includes both technical and creative aspects of your shoot:

▶ On the technical front, you need to review the essential equipment to bring to your shoot, as well as think about bringing extra, helpful items.

▶ On the creative front, you need to think about what shots you would ideally like to have in your finished movie. This chapter reviews what shots are most important to get and lists other shots that are "nice-to-haves."

A camera, a tripod, and a power supply are all you really need. But a few other items—especially extra batteries and a quick charger or car charger—can come in very handy.

If you're going to be traveling in your own car, a car charger for your camcorder is a good investment. If you're staying in hotel rooms, quick battery chargers are also very nice to have. You may have to charge your batteries daily, so get in the habit of plugging in your charger as soon as you get to your overnight lodgings.

If you are traveling with kids and want to splurge, bring along a few extra disposable camcorders and teach them how to shoot — sparingly, to make their 20-minute video supply last.

TIP

Are you going on a wild ride? Are you going to have an immersive experience? Let's say you're going on an amusement park ride or taking a rafting trip. You can strap on a disposable or sport camcorder and give your audience a front-row seat for the action. See Chapter 7, "Project 3: Making Sporting Event Movies" for more details.

Here is a list of essentials you should bring with you:

▶ Camcorder

▶ Videotape

▶ Tripod

▶ Power supply

▶ Fully charged batteries

▶ Extra charged batteries

▶ Your camera's power cord (for recharging batteries)

Here is a list of other equipment you should consider taking along:

▶ Car battery charger

▶ Quick battery charger

▶ External microphone for interviews

▶ Disposable camcorder(s)

▶ Sports camcorder

Shooting a Travel or Vacation Movie

Many travel movies are ho-hum; they have lots of nice scenery but don't really take advantage of video's unique ability to tell stories. You need to learn how to make the most of any situation to shoot great video.

In travel movies, shoot quickies —just 30 seconds here or a minute there—to get plenty of impressionistic shots. Get different angles and details of scenes. You'll want to have a good variety of shots from each scene to edit together into sequences.

For shooting exterior locations, set up your tripod and get (slow) pans and (extremely slow) zooms. Try a variety of speeds in panning and zooming so you'll have several choices in the editing stage.

Enjoy the sights and sounds of your trip and shoot what naturally attracts your attention. Shooting travel movies is like shooting a constantly moving target. Every day is a new day, and the experience of discovering special places is very satisfying—enriched by your ability to capture those impressions visually.

On other hand, don't overdo it. Have the trip you came for! Occasionally put the camera away and experience the trip without a digital dimension. You'll refresh your senses and bring more to your shooting when you pick up the camera again. Have fun exploring—and documenting—your appreciation of new experiences and horizons.

It's your big chance to play National Geographic television show producer. So consider what shots you need to get.

Variety is important in travel movies. You'll see lots of new things, so shoot frequently and broadly. One long shot of the cathedral won't be all that interesting when you go to edit your video. So shoot a wide shot—say, of a cathedral—and then shift to covering the details— the sculptures around the door, the tourists waiting in line outside, the fountain in the courtyard. You're painting a picture in time, so shoot different views of a single place.

Interviews—from your companions and from locals—will add human interest to your travel movie. It's often the "people experiences" on a trip that bring a place to life.

Like many other people, you may find that making great travel movies is fun and rewarding. If you get just a few of the shots from the following suggestions (see Figures 6.1 and 6.2), you'll have a movie that your friends and family will appreciate for years to come.

FIGURE 6.1

A wide shot of street vendors in Vietnam.

FIGURE 6.2

A medium shot of street vendors in Vietnam.

Shots to Get Before the Trip Begins

Your movie can begin the moment you begin planning your trip. Here are some creative ideas for capturing shots and sequences before the trip even begins.

Shooting Trip Planning

You can bring the camera out when you, your family, or a group are in the planning stages. Videotape some of the discussion of who would like to go where and why. After you've decided on a destination, you can videotape discussions of who's going to bring what (and why), especially on a camping trip. If you're traveling on a group tour and there's a pretrip get-together, shooting that will make a nice addition to your movie.

Shooting Getting Ready to Go

From packing scenes (what to bring?) to those pre-dawn departures, leaving home is filled with interesting scenes. The cab ride to the airport, the airport at sunrise—you don't have to wait until you've landed in Puerto Rico to start shooting.

Shooting Travel Vehicles

A shot of everyone getting in the car and driving away from your house can be the start of your movie. (Editing it later at high speed can be fun.) A guided tour of your car or van or the plane can also be entertaining.

Shots to Get During the Trip

Shooting during a long drive or flight is a good way to get people's reflections on their travels.

In a group, this may be the only time everyone is together (because they run in different directions as soon as you arrive somewhere).

When you watch TV, notice how often you see a driving/riding shot in a regular program (cop shows, reality TV shows, and more). In real life, it's an informal setting and can help you get more candid comments than in an interview.

Shooting Exteriors of Buildings

Vary the angles of your shots. Just as in still photography, your travel movie will benefit from a variety of shots when you edit it. Get a long shot of the exterior and details. You can also shoot several sides of a building that is architecturally noteworthy or do a walk-and-talk shot around different facades, zeroing in on any interesting features.

Scanning Famous (and Not-So-Famous) Works of Art

Many museums do not allow you to shoot their collections. If you want your movie to include images of world-famous paintings in the Louvre, buy postcards or books of the images, scan them, and edit these shots into your movie. Or shoot close-ups of posters or other images on location.

Getting On-location Narration

If you're walking around a location, describe what you're seeing, especially if there is a cultural angle. For instance, showing your viewers a row of snakes in jars on your trip to Vietnam is more interesting if you're talking about the snake wine, its medicinal qualities, and how everyone you met swears it works. If you don't fill in the details with audio, your audience won't understand why you shot it or what it means.

Recording Walk-and-Talk Shots

To take walk-and-talk shots, follow someone around as he or she walks and also talks to the camera. (You may have to learn how to walk backward or at least sideways to do this!) It's a great way to vividly capture the sense of a place and explore it at the same time, and it is intrinsically more interesting than someone standing still in a place. Try it and see what happens.

Shooting Food and Eating Scenes

Food is a subject everyone can relate to. Chances are you'll be eating something that reflects the local character of the place you're visiting. Even bad food can be interesting for people to talk about. Everyone has opinions.

Shooting sequences adds variety to movies. And food is always a good subject for a video sequence. Figures 6.3 through 6.8 show a series of shots from a friend's visit to Vietnam. See how much more interesting a variety of shots is and the different kinds of information each type of shot provides?

Interviewing People You Meet and Your Traveling Companions

Interact with people you meet and ask them if they will let you videotape them for a few minutes. People are usually interested in people who are interested in them and often have lots to say once you have established a connection.

Recording Daily Highlights

Interview your travel companions once a day about a favorite thing they saw that day. You can do this individually or in a group.

FIGURE 6.3
A wide shot of restaurant.

FIGURE 6.4
A medium shot of food.

FIGURE 6.5
**A medium shot of a
waitress.**

FIGURE 6.6

A close up shot of a waitress.

FIGURE 6.7

A close up shot of a meal.

FIGURE 6.8
A wide shot after a meal.

Shooting at Different Times of Day

Shoot in the early morning—when the streets are empty, the village is quiet, the sun is just beginning to light the town square, people are drinking coffee in the cafe. Shoot night scenes—people having dinner in restaurants, taxis driving by, people dancing in the streets. This will give you more texture and variety than if you shoot at the same time of day everyday.

Trying the "A Day in the Life of" Format

Often what makes a travel movie entertaining is a mix of little moments and big ones—not just the great landmarks, but also the best market, the taco vendor at the beach, surfers at sunset. Try shooting from dawn to night in one day in a place—or editing a sequence in your movie this way—to show a day from beginning to end.

Repeating a Theme or Question

Ask the same question of lots of people on your trip. It can be anything: from "What's your favorite food around here?" or "What's your favorite place to tell tourists to go?" to "What's your favorite view in this place?" Even just one question, asked of many different people along the trip, edited together makes a great running theme in a movie.

Capturing Running Gags: A Special Guest Star

You know how kids have stuffed animals they sleep with every night? A special friend can become a character in your travel movie, too.

Lest you think this is just for kids, check out the French movie *Amelie*. The main characters pose a red dwarf in many of the places they visit throughout the film. (Now Expedia is using this same motif in its ads.) Some artist friends of mine taking a trip across America used this same idea, posing a figurine and photographing it against the local scenery, to create a theme-based visual element.

Bring an imaginary character with you and set it up everywhere you go. Let your kids tell you what adventures it's had. It can even add spice and family fun to a rather ordinary road trip.

Shots to Get After Your Trip Is Over

After your journey, you can take more shots to tie together all your other footage. The following sections provide some suggestions.

Recording the Journey's End

Unpacking the suitcase or the car, rifling through the postcard collection, the bag with all the souvenirs you bought…all these are good scenes to have. Interview everyone in the family about the souvenirs they brought back and edit this into your movie.

TIP

Remember the slogan "lock and label" throughout your shoot. When you've finished shooting a tape, press the Record/Save tab to save to protect your valuable footage and be sure to label each tape you use.

Mapping Your Path

Using maps to tell the story of your journey helps make your travel movie special. Following are three ways to incorporate maps that will add extra entertainment value to your movie—using The Road Trip Effect, shooting maps, and using online maps from Google and MSN.

Would you like to add to your movie a free, beautifully animated map of your trip? Impress everyone who sees your movie by using The Road Trip Effect, one of my all-time favorite, free downloads, available at www.solrobots.com/roadtrip/index.html.

The Road Trip Effect lets you select a departure point and an arrival point, and then it animates that path, using NASA satellite photos of the world.

You can choose from plane, van, car, or ship icons to represent your travel mode; add multiple points; select different speeds of lines; and change the color or width of the lines. This program is really amazing.

When you select what you want, the program generates video you can edit into Movie Maker. If you like, you can then add music or narration in Movie Maker.

In contrast, a very low-tech way to add maps to movies is to shoot a map by using your camcorder and a tripod. You can highlight your journey with colored markers. If you mark your journey in small segments and shoot a take of each handmade "progress bar," you can edit this together in your movie to show the unfolding of the path.

Another low-tech way to incorporate maps is to shoot a daily map feature with your travel companions and, using a map in the shot, have them point out where you are today, where you came from, and where you're going on a daily basis. Be sure to get a few close-ups of the map (or shoot that when you get home).

Using satellite maps from online sites is another way to get digital images to edit into your travel movies. Use the satellite images at Google's maps www.maps.google.com and select the locations you want images of. (Microsoft has this feature, too.) For even slicker satellite mapping effects, check out Google Earth (at www.earth.google.com), which has a lot more features, including 3D drawings of major U.S. cities.

You can save a copy of any of these images on your PC by using the PrintScrn key, which is located in the upper right of most PC keyboards. Using this command saves a copy of the image to the clipboard, and you can then create a **.jpg** or other image file type, which you can then import into a collection in Movie Maker. Macintosh users can use the Grab feature in any version of Mac OS X to copy onscreen images.

You can save a series of images of the same location at different heights and edit cross-dissolves between the images to create the illusion of descending or ascending aerial views. You can also edit together a satellite view, dissolving into the regular map view in Google maps, or vice versa.

All these map effects are fun to play with and add a cool factor to your travel movies.

Editing Your Travel or Vacation Movie

After you shoot your footage, you should have lots of material to edit into great sequences in your travel movie.

If you have so much footage that you find it a bit overwhelming, you can break down your material into likely sequences, which makes a large volume of footage more manageable. You don't have to import all your video at once; you can just import 10- or 15-minute portions of a tape at a time, organize the material, and even edit it before continuing to import additional footage.

You can think through a variety of approaches to structuring your movie—including audio, visuals, people, and time. One approach is to consider whether you want audio to guide the structure your movie. Your options are to use music alone, part music and audio, or all audio. Editing a movie to music is usually pretty easy, so that's a good way to get started. But if you have great audio or interactions from your trip, you may want to create some sequences that have audio only interspersed with other music-only sequences. Of course you can also mix music under your audio, too.

You can also use *visuals* as a guide to organizing your footage, selecting the shots that are the best looking and that also tell the story of your adventure.

Using the most interesting characters and people moments is also a good way to cull the best material from your footage. This allows you to use your best bits from interviews of groups or individuals on camera.

Time is another way you can structure your movie: You have a beginning, middle, and end to your journey, so you can just start editing sequences from each stage of your trip.

Using a combination of all these approaches in structuring a movie will make your movie engaging and action packed.

In addition, you can add narration (which you can do by taping yourself, importing audio into your computer, and editing it in Movie Maker) to tell the story of the trip.

NOTE

If you don't have an audio microphone to record your narration directly into your computer, you can use your camcorder to record your narration and import it as a video in Movie Maker.

You may also decide to edit several versions of your footage, such as a highlights movie (with just music, if you like)—either on your own or with Movie Maker's AutoMovie feature—and an extended version.

Take your time when editing. After all, the trip is over, so there probably isn't a lot of pressure to finish your movie. On the other hand, getting a quick highlights movie done will give you some immediate gratification, momentum, and a feeling of accomplishment right away, which can propel you to the next stage of editing a longer, more detailed movie.

Basic Editing Steps

When you can take time to look at your footage, watch your tapes to see what portions you want to import. It's important to select only the best material so that you can create entertaining sequences.

As you work with your material, be diligent about editing out anything that doesn't work—either by trimming and tightening it up or by deleting it. Eventually, you will find the gems

FINDING THE PERFECT MUSIC FOR YOUR TRAVEL OR VACATION MOVIE

Adding great music to your travel and vacation movies will bring more personality and life to them. Finding the perfect music for your movies is easier than ever, using (legal, of course) free or low-cost music download sources on the Internet.

For travel and vacation movies, some of the best places to find music are on CD, at FreePlay Music (www.freeplaymusic.com; which offers hundreds of MP3 tracks to download for free—legally, of course), and at the Apple iTunes Music Store (www.apple.com/itunes; which offers 99¢ downloads).

Here are some of the best songs to add a special touch to your travel and vacation movie:

- "Don't Fence Me In" (Willie Nelson and others)
- "Love Trip" (Jerry Kilgore)
- "On the Road Again" (Rosemary Clooney, Willie Nelson, and others)
- "Road Trip" (Gary P. Nunn)

Special selections for kids on the Apple iTunes Music Store site are "Car Trip" (Jeffrey Friedberg) and "Road Trip" (Rebecca Frezza).

You can also use the additional sources in Chapter 3, "Editing Basics: Movie Maker and More" to create the perfect soundtracks for your travel and vacation movies.

in your footage and create sequences that polish those diamonds in the rough.

TIP

You can edit photos into your movie by using Movie Maker. For more information about adding motion to your photos, see Chapter 9, "Project 5: Making Family Memory Movies." The "Making an Advanced Slideshow Movie" section in Chapter 9 tells you how to use Microsoft's Photo Story 3 software to add pans and zooms (and other cool features) to still photos.

Here's a quick review of the steps outlined in Chapter 3:

1. Select the best portions of your footage and organize your coverage into sections that are roughly organized as a beginning, a middle, and an end.

2. Import the video into your computer and create and insert it in a Movie Maker collection.

3. Select the clips you like best and place them in the order in which you think they should go in the Timeline view or Storyboard view. Edit your shots into sequences.

4. Trim your clips.

5. Edit your clips together, using dissolves.

6. Add music.

7. Add titles.

8. Review your edited rough cut and evaluate it.

9. Review your edited fine cut and make any final changes.

10. Save, share, and enjoy your finished movie.

NOTE

Did you interview people during your trip, and you want to put them in your movie, but you never got their names? You can insert a title that's descriptive to inject humor into your movie (for example: "Man who told us wrong way to go").

Summary

Shooting travel movies makes your great adventures last longer; with these movies, you can enjoy reliving your travels when back at home. Shooting travel movies also trains your eye, as you learn to see things differently, and it provides a natural way to interact more with the people you meet and the places you go.

In this chapter, you've gotten a detailed overview of how to make travel movies that can truly captivate an audience, using shot lists with many suggestions for interesting material to shoot along the way.

Using the steps outlined in this chapter should help you avoid the most common mistakes in vacation movies:

▸ Boring static shots (because you learned how to shoot action and a mix of shots to build sequences from)

▸ Movies without interesting characters (because you've shot people—and perhaps food—along the way)

▸ Rambling edits that are unfocused (because you've learned how to apply several organizing principles to help structure your movie)

This chapter also provides online resources to help you find inspiring road or travel movies to watch, song titles and sites to help you find the perfect music, and ways to integrate animated maps into your movie that will make your finished movies fun to watch.

Using these techniques and resources can give you all you need to know to making travel movies that bring to the screen the amazing adventures you take. Now take this learning along with you every time you make a travel or vacation movie!

CHAPTER 7

Project 3: Making Sporting Event Movies

Sports is one of the easiest and best subjects for making great movies. The camera (like the human eye) loves motion, action, and dynamism—all of which most sports have plenty of. (That's why there are so many sports programs on TV.)

Sporting events have plenty of action—and conflict. Compelling dramas make engaging movies. In sports, someone is going to win, and someone is going to lose. That's inherently interesting.

In this chapter, we'll look at the best ways to capture the action and the emotion of a sports event, beginning with how to shoot. Shooting outdoor sports is fun because there's lots and lots of action—and color and emotion. As an added bonus, audio and lighting are often simpler in this kind of shooting than in shooting other kinds of movies.

You can also find information in this chapter about sports camcorders and disposable camcorders for capturing participatory, first-person shots to give your viewers the feeling that they are experiencing the action themselves.

This chapter provides editing tips, too, as well as editing resources—including selected sports music tracks, tips on using AutoMovie to make quick highlights movies, and how to use Movie Maker video effects to speed up or slow down action shots.

Creative Approaches to Making Sports Movies

Just as there are dozens of sports to cover, from football and soccer to surfing and kick boxing, there are many different kinds of movies about sports—from the basic sports game movie to the reality TV series. This section looks at some creative approaches you can take to making a sports movie, including hosting your own sports newscasts, starring in a sports movie, or making a season series.

Hosting your own sports show can be a lot of fun. Have you always secretly (or not so secretly) thought you could do better than the TV announcer who covers the football game? Well, this is your big chance to come out of the closet and onto the screen. Instead of being a Monday morning quarterback, you (or a friend) can narrate the movie during the shoot (or after). Consider working with a friend on being on-camera hosts, with plenty of back-and-forth banter and disagreements—like the two brothers on the radio show *Car Talk*.

TIP

The quickest and easiest way to make sportcaster movies is to use Vlog It! software from Serious Magic. You can edit in scenes from your own footage at a game as well as on-camera shots of yourself or a friend. For sportscasts, using Vlog It! is faster and simpler than using Movie Maker. For more information about Vlog It!, visit www.seriousmagic.com.

If you participate in a sport, think about starring in your own movie. If you're a skateboarder, dude, you could be the on-camera star (and/or host) as you show yourself and your friends doing your hottest tricks, making your own version of the X Games.

CREATIVE APPROACHES TO MAKING SPORTS MOVIES

TIP

For inspiration, you can watch the online trailer for the feature documentary *Dogtown and Z-Boys* on Yahoo! Movies, at http://movies.yahoo.com/shop?d=hv&cf=trailer&id=1804383683.

You can try using one of the new sports camcorders or a disposable camcorder to record the action, if you want to capture some first-person action shots without risking damage to your expensive camcorder.

If you're a parent (and the driver, for instance) who's going to be attending many games your child is playing in, you can make a movie about your son or daughter or the entire team for a whole season. Look for opportunities to make your own reality TV show.

TIP

For season series inspiration, rent the basketball documentary *Hoop Dreams*.

Making sports movies, like making other kinds of movies, is all about expressing your own creativity, and that can mean taking risks. What do you have to lose? If you don't like how a movie works out, well, you can just edit out what you don't like, slap on some cool music, and cut the action to the beat. Or you can perfect your on-camera act and do more takes. You'll find what works for you. The beauty of digital video is the ability to experiment and see what turns out to be magic onscreen.

SHOOTING FIRST-PERSON ACTION SHOTS

Want to capture the action of participating in (not just watching) a sport? You have two options to consider: shooting with a sports camcorder (which features a remote lens and mike you can strap on your body, along with the camera) and trying a disposable video camera. Let's say you're going snowboarding, and you want to shoot the action during your run. You can strap on a tiny sports camcorder (smaller than some cell phones) and position the external lens on your body—over your shoulder or anywhere else within a three-foot range of the camcorder. It will capture you (or your shoulder and the back of your head) as well as all the action. It's perfect for snowboarding, surfing, skydiving—whatever!

The first of these cameras to be released is the SC-X105L from Samsung (about $570). (To read David Pogue's *New York Times* article about this camcorder, visit www.nytimes.com/2005/06/09/technology/circuits/09pogue.html.) Small and rugged, this water-resistant camera lets you shoot up to 10 minutes of best-quality video or more at lower quality (about 60 minutes of webcam-quality record time).

You can also see David Pogue trying out the sports camcorder (see Figures 7.1 and 7.2). Use the Multimedia search (in advanced search) at www.nytimes.com and type in "Pogue Tries a Novel Camcorder" to find and play the movie.

Don't want to invest money in an expensive sports camcorder? Try one of the new disposable video cameras (about $29; available at CVS and elsewhere). The quality will be lower, but so will the price. Strap it onto your body, turn it on, and take off! You can shoot up to 20 minutes of footage and, for an additional fee,

continues

get it transferred to a DVD. You can import the DVD footage into your computer to edit it.

Integrating first-person action shots into your movie will add a whole new dimension to your sports movies that can "wow" your audience.

FIGURE 7.1
The *New York Times* tech columnist David Pogue gets wild and crazy with a sports camcorder in this clip from an online movie.

FIGURE 7.2
A close-up of Pogue's novel camcorder.

Any sports movie is easy to edit because you have a lot of options for cutting it—from making a highlights movie to showing the whole enchilada. It's easy to make highlights movies that show only the big action moments over racy music. On the other hand, coaches and athletes might want to watch every single minute of the game to learn and train. Seeing a movie of the event is often the only way athletes will see how they played and how the team as a whole performed.

To please a general audience, you should make an exciting, fast-paced, short highlights movie. Edit your shots over a rockin', amped-up music track, and you'll end up with a cool movie. Ah, the magic of editing! Are you ready to get started now?

Getting Ready for Your Shoot

Your sports movie begins with the right preparation, including both the technical and creative aspects of your shoot:

▶ On the technical front, you need to review the essential equipment to bring to your shoot, as well as think about bringing extra, helpful items.

▶ On the creative front, what shots would you ideally like to have in your finished movie? We'll review what shots are most important to get and a list of other shots that are "nice-to-haves." Do you need to shoot the whole event? Or just the parts where your son, daughter, or other favorite athlete is playing? We'll review what shots are most important to get and a list of other shots to think about.

It's important that you bring the right stuff to your shoot. For sports events, you can use one camera and a tripod.

Use your tripod. You won't be happy if all you bring home is jerky shots of the winning moment. If you're shooting an entire game, you'll get tired of holding the camera for that length of time. On the other hand, if you only want to capture a few minutes (a swim meet, for instance), you could probably get by without a tripod—but you might still be happier if you had one.

Another great piece of equipment that will help you run around the field and get hand-held action shots is a camcorder shoulder brace. Professional models are expensive (more than $600), but a few consumer models have come onto the market recently that sell for about $150. You can search online for suppliers.

You can also consider bringing a second camera (or more) and cameraperson. The next time you watch a sports event on TV, see how many camera angles (and camera positions) a typical big game program has. If, for instance, you are shooting a big swim meet and others can help you shoot, ask someone else to bring his or her camcorder along and be a second cameraperson. If you're taping a school sports event, and other parents on your child's team show up with their camera every week, too, you could piggyback on each other's efforts and take different positions during events, trading footage afterward. Shooting with two cameras can add a lot to sports coverage.

You need to think about your power supply ahead of time. Will you be shooting with batteries, or will you need to plug into the power on location? It's important to make sure your batteries are charged. You should also bring extra charged batteries so you can make it through the whole game.

Another power alternative is to use your camera's power cord for indoor games. If you're using your power cord and an electric outlet at an event, you need to bring an extension cord and duct tape (to cover your cord to make sure no one trips over it).

If you're going to be shooting a whole season of games and will be on the road, traveling to and from games, a car charger for your batteries might be a good investment.

The audio for your shoot is another consideration. Shooting sports is usually an easy audio situation. For most of the event, the visual action is the main focus.

However, in a basketball game or another indoor sport, or where there is an announcer, you may want to get the audio. Usually your camera-mounted mike will be enough to handle this.

On the other hand, if you're in the stands at a football game, your camera mike is going to capture the sounds closest to you (like the people yelling and screaming when their team scores a touchdown). This may or may not be the sound you want. If it's someone buying popcorn from a vendor, or if you and a friend are gabbing away, that's the audio you'll be hearing when you edit your movie. (Of course, you can use music to cover it—a common fix.) The point is that you need to be aware that the audio you hear while you're holding your camera is the audio you're going to get unless you edit it out.

Here is a list of essentials you should bring with you to shoot the sporting event:

- ▶ Camcorder
- ▶ Videotape
- ▶ Tripod
- ▶ Power supply
- ▶ Fully charged batteries
- ▶ Extra charged batteries
- ▶ Your camera's power cord (for recharging batteries)

Here is a list of other equipment you should consider taking with you:

- ▶ Car battery charger
- ▶ Quick battery charger
- ▶ Extra batteries
- ▶ External microphone for interviews
- ▶ Disposable camcorder(s)
- ▶ Sports camcorder
- ▶ Duct tape (to cover audio extension cords or power cords)

Shooting Your Sports Movie

Shooting sports is all about location, location, location—being in the right spot to capture the action. When the game begins, you may be able to move around on a field, for instance, but if you're in the stands, you may not be able to grab your gear to get to where the action is. You should find the best spot or spots where you'll be able to get an overall view of the action. Over time, because fields are pretty similar, you'll get a feeling for the best positions.

When you're in a good spot, you may be able to stay there for the entire event. Or you may choose to roam around during the action, to get great shots from a number of locations and angles.

The big win in sports movies is having your camera pointed at the action when it happens. That sounds easy, but in some sports (such as baseball), it can be a little tricky because you may find yourself waiting, waiting, waiting—and then bingo! The big play happens! It takes patience and stamina to wait for that big moment and act at the right time. This is one situation where you may need to zoom in (or out) fast!

How much you plan the shots you would like to have depends on how casual or important the event is. If it's a Little League baseball game, you can probably be pretty casual in your approach. If it's a big college swim meet and your daughter is contending for a spot on the Olympic team, you may want to prepare more.

For major events, one option is to shoot a meet before the one you're really interested in to figure out the best angles and locations, where the audio will be coming from, where to connect to power outlets in the building, and other details that can increase your chances of shooting the best footage. When the big event comes, you can rewind your tape and reuse it (or don't actually record the rehearsal). With your personal dress rehearsal behind you, you'll be able to focus more on shooting the action and less on technical details.

In sports, it's always a good idea to be able to quickly and easily switch back and forth between shooting on a tripod and shooting handheld footage. You should practice getting your camera on and off the tripod so this motion starts to come naturally to you. And don't forget that you can run around the field with your camera still mounted on your tripod, too. (Just try not to hit anyone with it accidentally!)

Remember to vary your shots, to get wide, medium, and close-up shots, as shown in Figures 7.3 and 7.4.

FIGURE 7.3
Wide shot of a golfer.

FIGURE 7.4
Medium shot of the subject.

You should also think about camera movement. Because sports events are full of motion, you need to follow the action with your camera, while maintaining stable shots and controlled zooms and pans. There's that word again—*controlled*. Remember not to pan and zoom too fast or too often, and you'll be fine.

ESPN crews have cameras in many different spots throughout a location. (For fun, try watching a sports show and counting the number of camera views.) Do you have this luxury? No. Can your movie be just as entertaining? Yes. How? Because you can run around and get the same human interest interviews the pros do—with coaches, athletes, fans, and anyone else who might have something interesting to say about the game, the sport, or a player.

So pay attention to the following shot list and go for the gold! Your goal is to put yourself in situations that maximize your chances of scooping up the best of what's there.

Shots to Get Before the Event

Starting to shoot your sports movie before the event begins will help you tell more of the whole story about the event (and not just the action on the field) and build a sense of anticipation.

Shooting Scenes of Getting Ready to Go to the Event

You could shoot your athlete waking up in the morning, getting dressed, putting on his uniform, eating, gathering his equipment, and getting packed to go to the event. You can ask your star what he's thinking about this game—his hopes and fears. What technique is he hoping to improve? What are his physical and mental preparation? This type of shot will add a lot of human interest.

Shooting Traveling to the Event

There's a lot of camaraderie and team spirit on the rides to and from sporting events. If you ride on the bus (maybe you're even on the team), you can shoot interviews with the coach, the team, and supporters. What's going to be the biggest challenge the team faces with these particular opponents? What has the team been working on in practice that it hopes to execute during the game?

The advantage of shooting en route is that your interviewees are held captive in a confined space of a vehicle and may be more accessible than when they get to the event. The disadvantage is that the bus may be very noisy (and bumpy). Do the best you can. (Sometimes you have to politely ask people to be quiet for a minute or two while you get a quick comment.)

Shooting the Location

When you arrive at the event, you can shoot some of the local color. Is there a sign announcing the name of the town or the name of the high school? You can shoot the empty field or the exterior of the building. You only need a few seconds, but having these shots will help make your movie more interesting and set the stage for the action to come.

Shooting Scenes in the Locker Room or Outside

Ask the coach and team whether you can shoot some locker room prep scenes (if you are the same sex as the athletes). It's best to shoot from the chest up (so as to avoid showing overly personal body parts) unless everyone is clothed. If you've cleared it ahead of time with the coach and the team, you might want to shoot the coach's pregame pep talk or instructions (inside or outside the locker room). Later you can edit out anything that's not appropriate to include.

Shooting Scenes of the Athletes Going onto the Field

A nice shot to get is one of all the players going by you as they run out onto the field. Remember that the *camera* stays *still* and the *players run* by. You can put titles over this footage later when you edit your movie, as they do in pro football games on TV. Have some fun!

Shooting Fan Scenes

Your movie will be much more fun if you interact with people and capture that on camera (instead of staying a safe distance away all the time). Video is a much more engaging way of documenting events than taking still photos. But you need to be sure to be friendly and polite. You should ask people whether it's okay to videotape them, and you need to respect their privacy if they don't want to be involved.

While you're waiting around for the event to begin, you can shoot whatever else is happening. Ask people around you who they are and why they came to this event. Shoot a down-the-line shot of people standing in line. Shoot ticket taking and ticket takers. Ask people what they're hoping to see today. Shoot tailgate picnics and anything else that might be entertaining.

If someone is selling ice cream, you can get a shot of that and ask the seller about today's game. Don't worry if people give you dull comments. They may say something priceless in the very next sentence. This is more common than you think, and it's one of the things that makes shooting (and editing) fun! Dull stuff winds up on the cutting room floor, and cool stuff makes it into your edited movie. Your job while shooting is to scoop it all up because you can sort it out later. Don't feel bad if you only get great stuff from every tenth person—that's par for the course.

Look for people whose appearance suggests a larger-than-life personality—people wearing outrageous fan attire or funny hats, carrying signs, and so on. These are visual cues that they have something to express and will make potentially more engaging comments on video in a very quick grab-and-go shooting situation. Of course, this is a generalization, and you may find a wealth of wisdom, knowledge, and humor from anyone you meet, but if you're looking for the low-hanging fruit, scoop up the obvious.

Shots to Get During the Event

The main point of your sports movie is to shoot the event, and here are some shots you need to be sure to include.

Shooting the Opener

You should be sure to shoot the start of the game or event—the kickoff, the race gun, the opening move. You gotta have it.

Shooting the Game

You should try to get the game from several different angles, and you should reframe throughout the game from wide shots to medium and closer shots and back to wide shots. If there are breaks in the action, you can move from one location to another to vary your views of the game, if you want to. You might want to avoid having the same view from the same location for the whole game, unless you're moving your shot in and out and shooting well. You should make the most of the opportunities you have, as I have done in Figure 7.5.

Shooting Brief Half-Time Interviews

If they don't mind, check in with your star, the coach, or the team and tape them during a break. You may want to be more unobtrusive than you were before the game; you need to be sensitive to a player's or a team's concentration and focus as well as their need for downtime during their break.

This is also a good time to shoot fan scenes and commentary. How did your bleacher mates think the team did during the first half? What are their observations about various plays and players?

FIGURE 7.5
"The game" can be the action in front of your house.

TIP

Remember the slogan "lock and label" throughout your shoot. When you've finished shooting a tape, press the Record/Save tab to save to protect your valuable footage and be sure to label each tape you use.

Shots to Get After the Event

Whether your team or player won or lost, there will be plenty of emotion to capture after the event. Here are some shots you need to be sure to get.

Shooting Locker Room or Other Shots of the Players

Victory is easy to shoot because no one minds being a winner. Shoot everything! But if your side lost, you need to be more sensitive about shooting. Unless you're shooting a seasoned pro, you need to give defeat some time to sink in; you may get better material after people have a little bit of time to reflect.

If your team lost, there's still a lot you can ask the team members: What did they learn from the challenge of the event? What did they think would happen? What surprised them?

You need to be aware of your own feelings: You should try to be impartial and nonjudgmental and not communicate any feelings of disappointment to your interviewees during interviews, if they lost. On the other hand, if your subjects were victorious, you can share their enthusiasm!

Shooting an Interview with Your Favorite Athlete

The aftermath of a competition is a great time to capture the emotion of the moment. This is a good time to shoot an interview with your favorite still-sweaty athlete.

Shooting Fan Comments and Scenes

You should shoot things that suggest the mood: from waving flags and singing to the team getting back on the bus and driving away. If you're on the bus, you can shoot whatever is naturally happening—singing, philosophical musings, silence.

Another way to go is to ask someone to interview you about shooting that day or about the

FINDING THE PERFECT MUSIC FOR YOUR SPORTS MOVIE

Adding great music to your sports movies will bring more personality and life to them. Finding the perfect music for your movies is easier than ever, using (legal, of course) free or low-cost music download sources on the Internet.

For sports movies, some of the best places to find music are on CD, at FreePlay Music (www.freeplaymusic.com; which offers hundreds of MP3 tracks to download for free—legally, of course), and at the Apple iTunes Music Store (www.apple.com/itunes; which offers 99¢ downloads).

Here are some of the best songs to add a special touch to your sports movie:

- ▶ *Chariots of Fire* theme (Vangelis and others)
- ▶ *Star Wars* main theme (John Williams)
- ▶ *Raiders of the Lost Ark* theme (John Williams)
- ▶ *Mission Impossible* theme (Danny Elfman and others)
- ▶ *Bonanza* theme (Billy Strange)
- ▶ *Batman* theme (David McCallum)

You can also use the additional sources in the sidebar "Music Downloads for Movies" in Chapter 3, "Editing Basics: Movie Maker and More" to find the perfect soundtrack for your sports movie.

Movie Maker's video effects provide powerful ways to edit your footage, allowing you to play with time and motion.

You've seen instant replays on TV—the ones where the action slows way down so you can watch a player's technique or big moment—right? Well, envy the ESPN gods no more. With digital editing on your computer, you can achieve those same technological heights when it comes to slowing down or speeding up shots. For sports, what could be more fun?

Got a great play that you want to watch in slow motion? If so, in Movie Maker, select Collections, Video Effects, Slow Down, Half to preview the effect. Like this effect? Drag the icon onto your clip to apply it. You can keep applying the effect (up to six times) to make a 10-second clip into one that lasts up to 10 minutes, 40 seconds.

Got a long, boring part of a game on video but want to have some fun with it? Make it go twice as fast (or more) by selecting Collections, Video Effects, Speed Up, Double to preview it. Drag the icon onto your clip to apply it. If you want your clip to go even faster, you can keep applying the effect (up to six times) to make 10 seconds become 0.15625 seconds.

You should plan to put music over these shots (unless you want your original audio to play at a garbled fast or slow speed).

You can also use cool video effects to flip or rotate your video. You can choose from flipping the image (Mirror, Vertical, or Horizontal) or rotating (Rotate 90, Rotate 180, or Rotate 270) it to make gravity and time get wacky. The effect might express, for example, the way your snowboarding moves make you feel.

game, for instance, and have that person ask you the same questions. Or you can have someone shoot you and your interviewer, both on camera.

Editing Your Sports Movie

After you shoot your footage, you need to edit it into a sports movie. In general, structuring a sports movie is not that complicated because you usually want to follow the chronological order in which you shot the footage to tell the story.

Basic Editing Steps

When you can take time to look at your footage, watch your tapes to see what portions you want to import. It's important to select only the best material so that you can create action-packed movies.

As you work with your material, be ruthless about editing out anything that doesn't work—either by trimming and tightening it up or by deleting it. Eventually, your best footage will surface, and you can polish it until it shines. It's all about the content, right? Action, action! Or emotion, emotion!

You should take your time in editing, or you can make an AutoMovie of your footage if you want some instant gratification. If you're making both an AutoMovie and a longer version, you can share a brief highlights movie online and then focus on making a longer version that uses all your *best* material.

TIP

If you use the AutoMovie Sports Highlights style, Movie Maker will add pans and zooms to your footage, in addition to editing it to a music track.

Here's a quick review of the editing steps outlined in Chapter 3:

1. Select the best portions of your footage and organize your coverage into sections that are roughly organized as a beginning, a middle, and an end.

2. Import the video into your computer and create and insert it in a Movie Maker collection.

3. Select the clips you like best and place them in the order in which you think they should appear in the Timeline view or Storyboard view. Edit your shots into sequences.

4. Trim your clips.

5. Edit your clips together and apply video effects. Be adventurous with effects, if you like. Sports movies provide a good opportunity to use varied transitions. Evaluate the transitions you choose. Using too many wacky transitions can become predictable and tiresome.

6. Add music.

7. Add titles.

TIP

In sports movies you can get creative with titles by doing things like having them fly in. You can preview some of the interesting title motions to see what you like best. Movie Maker even has a title option called Sports Scoreboard. Refer to Chapter 3 for more information.

You can preview each of these effects by choosing them after you select Collections, Video Effects. You apply a video effect by dragging its icon onto your clip in the Storyboard or Timeline view. For more details on Movie Maker's video effects, see Chapter 3.

8. Review your edited rough cut and evaluate it.

9. Review your edited fine cut and make any final changes.

10. Save, share, and enjoy your finished movie.

Summary

In this chapter, you've learned about shooting a sports movie, using the shot lists of things to shoot at a sports event—from before the game to after the final scores are recorded. You've learned how to capture first-person shots, which you might want to incorporate into your movie. This information about shooting will ensure that you have great material to edit.

You've also learned about editing tips and techniques—including video effects and suggested music selections—to add energy and dynamism to your sports movies.

Using the steps outlined in this chapter should help you avoid the most common mistakes in sports movies:

▶ Static visuals (because you're changing your angles and shots)

▶ Boring footage that doesn't capture the emotion of the story (because you're doing lots of people interviews)

▶ Slow-paced editing (because you've learned how to delete or tighten up shots and sequences)

The more you shoot and edit, the more you'll learn. Sports events happen all the time, which means you have plenty of opportunity to get more experience.

Using these techniques and resources will help you become a better movie maker when it comes to shooting and editing sports movies people will want to watch. You now have everything you need to know to make your sports movies your "personal best."

CHAPTER 8

Project 4: Making School Play (and Other Live Event) Movies

Making a movie of a live event—such as a school play, recital or concert, or a theater or dance performance—preserves the performance long after the stage has gone dark. If you are planning to videotape a wedding, this chapter will help you, too, because covering weddings is similar to shooting other live events.

This chapter provides inspirational examples of many different types of creative approaches to making live event movies, along with detailed shot lists to help you explore the many opportunities you have for shooting a complete story about a live event, if you want to capture all the emotion and action behind-the-scenes as well as onstage.

Remember, the "magic" of creating a great performance movie depends on how well you capture the event when you're shooting so that you have great footage to edit. The best event movies capture not only the action onstage but scenes before and after, too. Adding a lot of "color" makes the difference between a ho-hum movie of a darkly lit stage and a fun, lively movie that brings back all the emotion of the original event.

This chapter includes a review of the editing process to help you turn your good footage into a dynamic, action-packed live event movie.

When you've finished shooting and editing your movie, you can share the finished movie with the "stars" on videotape, DVD, or the Web. For the performer, having a movie of the event is often the only way to see how the performance looked to the audience.

Creative Approaches to Making Live Event Movies

Just as there are different kinds of performances, there are many different types of movies you can make about an event. Of course, you can just shoot what happens onstage, but there is much more to the story. There are a number of approaches that movie makers and television producers have applied to make live event movies more compelling. You can use these techniques, too, if you want to expand the scope of your project.

If your stars are children in a school play, you're almost guaranteed to make a great movie. Children have a lot of energy, which the camera loves. Kids are wonderful to shoot, they express themselves naturally, and they are full of surprises. People naturally enjoy watching kids in movies—as long as the movie is edited well.

The popular feature documentaries *Mad Hot Ballroom* and *Spellbound* (see Figure 8.1) are wildly successful examples of using real-life children as stars in live event movies. You can rent these movies for inspiration and to educate yourself about the creative possibilities.

Would you make a good host in a movie? If so, you can consider putting yourself in front of the camera. For a little tongue-in-cheek movie, you could put together a panel of "judges" à la *American Idol*. You can have your friends perform for fun to make an entertaining movie.

Are you going to be in a performance? If so, you might want to make a movie about your creative process—from practice to performance.

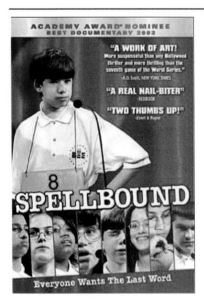

FIGURE 8.1

The popular feature documentaries *Mad Hot Ballroom* and *Spellbound*.

A first-person take on the performing arts could be just what the world is waiting for.

Rehearsal recordings can also be exciting to make and watch because they give the movie maker more room to maneuver and get behind-the-scenes. Performers may want to have a rehearsal videotaped before a show so they can polish their act before going onstage. You can help by shooting the rehearsal so they can fine-tune their production.

For inspiration, you can watch the Academy Award–winning documentary *In the Shadow of the Stars*. This movie (see Figure 8.2) takes you backstage at San Francisco's Opera, where it follows the lives of the chorus members.

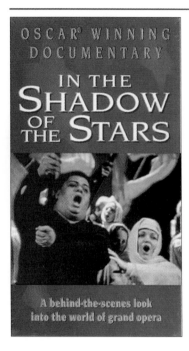

FIGURE 8.2

The Academy Award–winning documentary *In the Shadow of the Stars*.

Making a good live event movie is an art form unto itself, but one that anyone can learn. You, too, can shoot as if your movie were going to air on the E! television network.

Getting Ready for Your Shoot

Your movie begins with the right preparation, including both the technical and creative aspects of your shoot:

▶ On the technical front, you need to review the essential equipment to bring to your shoot, as well as think about bringing extra, helpful items.

▸ On the creative front, what shots would you ideally like to have in your finished movie? We'll review what shots are most important to get and a list of other shots that are "nice-to-haves."

If this is your first time videotaping a live event, you can use one camera, a tripod, and perhaps a shotgun mike or an external mike. This is the simplest setup, and with it you can get plenty of good footage.

A tripod is essential. You don't want to see wobbly shots of your star in her big moment. After you've used a tripod, you will wonder how anyone could shoot an event without one. You are likely to get tired of holding a camera for an entire performance. On the other hand, if your "star" is a six-year-old and the "performance" is a 5- to 10-minute classroom play, you may be able to get by without one.

For important occasions, you may need an external microphone to capture the sound. When you shoot live events, you often cannot get close to the performers, so you may need to have an external mike (a shotgun mike is best) because it's better than your regular camera-mounted mike at capturing audio from a distance. A less desirable solution is to mount an external microphone closer to the action; it will need to connected (by an audio extension cord) to your camera.

Here is a list of essentials you should bring with you to shoot the live event:

▸ Camcorder

▸ Videotape (removing the plastic wrapping ahead of time will save you time and aggravation during your shoot)

▸ Tripod

▸ Power supply

▸ Fully charged batteries or your camera's power cord

Here is a list of other equipment you should consider taking with you:

▸ Directional/shotgun or other external microphone

▸ Long audio extension cord to connect the external microphone to your camera

▸ Duct tape (to cover audio extension cords or power cords)

▸ Extra charged batteries

▸ A second camcorder, tripod, and power supply if you want to have continuous coverage of a formal performance (to cover any breaks when a tape ends)

Shooting Your Live Event Movie

How much you plan your shots depends on how casual or important the event is. If it's an elementary school play, you can probably be low key in your approach. If it's a very special occasion, such as your music major daughter's college piano recital or a wedding, you need to plan your shoot in more detail.

The pressure in a live event is that, as they say in show business, the show must go on. Events force you—like the performers—to be on your toes.

As you get ready to shoot the event, it's a good idea to make a list of shots to consider. This list should help you anticipate ahead of time where the action will be and help you get it at the right time. You can look for the emotion and the opportunities as they happen. That's the fun part. You should plan to improvise. Unless you're psychic, no shoot ever goes exactly as planned. There will be moments you hope to find and don't, and there will be many happy surprises. Your goal is to put yourself in situations that maximize your chances of scooping up the best of what's there.

If you're shooting a major event, such as a wedding or an important theatrical perform-ance, one option is to shoot a rehearsal so you know when important moments are about to happen, what the audio sounds like from different places in the room, when the lights are to go on and off, where to connect to power outlets in the building, and other details that might seem trivial but become important when you're making a movie. Knowing these details in advance relieves some of the stress of getting yourself set up on the day of the event. Of course, you need to strike a comfortable balance between being attentive to details and enjoying yourself. Making movies is fun, right?

Shots to Get Before the Event Begins

Your movie can begin with shots taken well in advance of the actual live event. Here are some creative ideas for capturing shots and sequences before the show begins.

Shooting Practicing Scenes

You should get some shots of your talent prac-ticing before the event. You can shoot prepara-tion leading up to the performance and find out what your star is thinking about. He or she will be more relaxed at this point than on the day of the performance.

Shooting Preshow Interviews

Interviewing your star or the director about her creative process is a great topic to explore well in advance of the event. You can interview several key people in a production about their impressions.

> **TIP**
>
> The DVD version of the Academy Award–winning film *Amadeus* provides a behind-the-scenes extra: an hour-long documentary on the making of the film, including a number of brilliant interviews about the director and writer's creative process. You can watch it to better understand the enter-tainment value of interviews about the creative process.

Shooting Exteriors of the Building at the Event

What is the setting for the live event? Can you get a good shot of the exterior? You should get out your tripod and shoot a slow pan or zoom of the building. Be sure to get some static shots (no panning, zooming, or pulling out). You only need a few seconds of this in your edited program, but these shots are nice to have. You might want to put titles over them and put them at the beginning of your movie.

Shooting a Sign or Poster Announcing the Event

You can title your movie in editing, but if you have a nice stable shot of something advertis-ing the event, you can use that footage instead of a title you create.

Shooting a Brief Interview with Your Star or Others at the Event

Having your star pose in front of the event's sign or poster and talk about the event can become a great sequence when you get to the editing room. You can also videotape parents, teachers, or the director about the event before the performance starts. It's fun to hear what they're thinking about before the show, and it can be a nice sequence when you edit the video.

Shooting Ticket Takers Taking Tickets

Scenes such as showing ticket takers collecting audience tickets enhance the sense of anticipation for the performance.

Shooting Scenes of the Audience Waiting to Enter

You can shoot a down-the-line shot by holding your camera steadily against your body or braced in your hands and walking down the line of people queued up to see the event. You might also ask some of them why they're there or what they're hoping to see.

Shooting the Audience Entering or People Waiting for the Performance to Begin

When you enter the place where the event is to take place, you should shoot a wide shot and a few close-ups. You can also pan down a row of people's faces. This is easy to do while you are set up with your tripod in the room and waiting for the show to begin. You'll probably only use a few seconds of this in your edited program, but it's good material.

Shooting Backstage Getting-Ready Scenes

Shooting backstage as those taking part in the event are getting ready is a great opportunity to capture a part of the event that the audience will not have seen—putting on costumes and makeup, last-minute instructions from a teacher or the director, and so on. You might be able to grab a quick interview with the director and/or stars about getting ready for the event, what they're looking forward to, or other comments about their hopes, fears, or preparation for the performance.

> **TIP**
>
> Remember the slogan "lock and label" throughout your shoot. When you've finished shooting a tape, press the Record/Save tab to save to protect your valuable footage and be sure to label each tape you use.

Shots to Get During the Performance

The main point of a live event movie is to shoot the performance, so you need to be sure to get coverage of the main event. You should include wide shots of the performance as well as stable close-ups of performers, if you can. You should also try to get some medium shots of interactions between performers. You should also try to frame a few close-up shots and remember to allow for enough headroom in your shots.

If you pan or zoom, remember to use the Widen/Tighten camcorder controls slowly and steadily for best results. But of course, for many informal events, just shooting the performance on one static shot is fine.

You should try to be unobtrusive during shooting so the audience enjoys the event without being distracted by you and the camera.

Overall, you should avoid too much camera motion. You should frame your shot and stay with it unless the action moves out of the frame. If the action does move out of the frame, pan or zoom out slowly to reframe the shot to include all the action.

If you are changing from one shot to another, change the shot as quickly as possible, reframe it, and stay on the newly reframed shot. If there is a break in the action, you can take that opportunity to change your shot if you want to reframe. You can also take advantage of a break in the action to move the camera and tripod to another location in the room if you want to vary your coverage. If you reposition yourself, you should try to do it during an intermission or some break so you can avoid distracting the audience from the performance.

Shots to Get After the Event

After the curtain falls, you have plenty of opportunities to capture the energy and emotion that follow the performance. You should try to get some of the shots described in the following sections.

Shooting Audience Interviews About the Performance

Emotions can run high at the end of a performance, so this is an especially good time to capture the energy the event has inspired.

I made a movie of my friend Jenny's six-year-old son's (Adrian) first-grade performance. Even the simplest school play movie may be the first time a six-year-old has even been videotaped, and it's a thrill for your "star" to watch himself or herself with friends and family members.

Figures 8.3 through 8.8 illustrate shooting a simple elementary classroom play, using the shooting suggestions described in this chapter: shots of the performance (including wide shots and a few close-ups), audience shots during the performance, "backstage" parent and star interviews, and a fan scene (autograph signing) after the performance.

FIGURE 8.3
During the event: Adrian "Live"!

continues

FIGURE 8.4
During the event: Adrian's close-up.

FIGURE 8.5
During the event: Parents watching the show.

Shooting the Performers and/or Your Star Backstage

You can shoot the performers, the audience, and the director or teacher after the performance. These might be the most fun sequences in your movie.

Shooting Fan Scenes

If you are a parent, you might want to have someone tape you, too. It's good to be in your own movies—at least for cameo appearances. You can also shoot autograph signings and other fan scenes.

Shooting is always an exercise in improvisation, and your subjects respond to the emotion you bring to the event. So you need to be relaxed and have fun with the process. No shoot ever goes exactly the way you planned it, and you can only shoot what's there. Unless you have insurmountable technical difficulties, you'll have some footage to edit, and if you keep shooting events, you'll find out what works best for you over time.

Editing Your Live Event Movie

After you shoot all kinds of great coverage, you can start editing your footage into sequences.

What makes an event movie easier to edit than many other kinds of movies is that an event has a built-in beginning, middle, and end. As a general rule, you can edit your footage in the order in which it was shot. Or you can make two separate movies: one of the performance and one that could be called "The Making of" that includes all the backstage scenes, interspersed with some of the performance shots.

Basic Editing Steps

When you can take time to look at your footage, you should watch your tapes to see what portions you want to import.

As you work with your material, you need to be diligent about editing out anything doesn't work—either by trimming and tightening it up or by deleting it. Because shooting a live event is sometimes tricky technically, you need to evaluate your footage for visual and sound quality:

▶ Is the lighting at a certain point so dark that the scene doesn't maintain interest? Or is something so interesting happening that the lighting doesn't really matter?

▶ Is the audio audible and loud enough? Or was the microphone not able to pick up the sound?

Don't be afraid to edit out anything that can't be heard well, if you want to delete it.

Here's a quick review of the editing steps outlined in Chapter 3, "Editing Basics: Movie Maker and More":

1. Select the best portions of your footage and organize your coverage into sections that are roughly organized as a beginning, a middle, and an end.

2. Import the video into your computer and create and insert it in a Movie Maker collection.

3. Select the clips you like best and place them in the order in which you think they should appear in the Timeline view or Storyboard view. Edit your shots into sequences.

4. Trim your clips.

5. Edit your clips together, using dissolves.

FIGURE 8.6
After the event: "Backstage" interview with Adrian's mom.

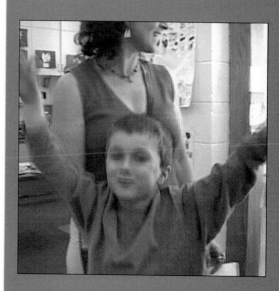

FIGURE 8.7
After the event: "Backstage" interview with Adrian.

continues

FIGURE 8.8
After the event: Adrian signing autographs.

A performance as short as five minutes can become an eight-minute DVD with multiple chapters. For example, inside the "Class Song" chapter of the DVD *Adrian's Really Big Show* are the following three subchapters:

▶ Class Singing Song (~4:00)

▶ Interview with Mom (with son embracing Mom and jumping up and down in front of the camera) (~2:00)

▶ Autograph Signing (kids signing autographs for each other on the flyer for the event) (~2:00)

6. Add music.

7. Add titles.

NOTE

If you have a shot of a flyer or poster for the event, you might use that as an opening title instead of creating a title in Movie Maker. Closing credits can also be entertaining—especially for your stars—and give you a place to include everyone's name, if you want to.

8. Review your edited rough cut and evaluate it.

9. Review your edited fine cut and make any final changes.

10. Save, share, and enjoy your finished movie.

Summary

In this chapter, you've learned that shooting live events can be as simple as videotaping an elementary school's class performance—or something much more complex—depending on the event and what you want your movie to be.

In this chapter, you've been introduced to some of the creative approaches you can take and explored extensive shot lists that provide many suggestions for what to shoot to get lots of life into your live event movies. And you've reviewed shots from a sample movie project that demonstrate how these shooting suggestions can be applied to create a simple movie.

This chapter also suggests several movies you can rent to better understand how professional movie makers have taken live events of everyday characters and situations and made them into compelling works of art—sometimes even winning Academy Awards!

Using the steps outlined in this chapter should help you avoid the most common mistakes in live event movies:

- Unintended shaky cam (because you've learned to use a tripod)
- Too many zooms in and zooms out (because you've learned to use the Widen/Tighten control sparingly, if at all)
- Poor audio (because miking the scene is especially important in live event movies)

Shooting a live event can be fun and easy—and it gets even simpler over time. The more events you shoot, the more you'll learn how to shoot and how to edit.

You can be proud of what you've learned—and chances are, your audience will thank you for it!

CHAPTER 9

Project 5: Making Family Memory Movies

In this chapter, you'll learn how to make family memory movies that preserve and protect your family's history.

A family memory movie can be anything from a simple photo slideshow of old family photos edited over music and saved as a digital movie to a deluxe family tree DVD with photos, audio, and/or video from each family member. It can be a birthday present—for a 75th birthday party, for instance—or a memorial to honor someone who has passed away.

Of all the projects in this book, creating a family memory movie may be one of the most satisfying. With this kind of movie, you have a built-in audience—your family—and a lot of great material to draw from, including family photos, audio recordings, old movies, VHS videos, and digital video clips.

This chapter covers making different kinds of family memory movies, including photo slideshow movies (using family photos) and tips on shooting new footage, including oral history interviews of a relative and family reunions.

In addition, in this chapter you'll find valuable information about gathering additional resources you can add to your treasure trove—suggestions on great music to edit into your movies, information on finding historical photos online to edit into your movie, and instructions on how to transfer VHS tapes to digital video files on miniDV tape (which you can then edit on a computer). Options for saving VHS tapes directly onto DVDs are also included.

Getting Ready to Make a Family Memory Movie

Family history is precious—and photos and movies of it are fragile—so making a family memory movie is a special gift to everyone in your family, possibly even for generations to come. You not only putting it all together for everyone to enjoy, but you also preserve it in a digital format that won't deteriorate over time. Whereas photos can fade and VHS video starts to decay within as little as 15 years, a digital version of your family's precious media will protect these important personal images.

You could just digitize your photos and VHS videos and archive them safely on a CD or DVD. But you will be doing yourself and your family a favor if you organize your material and edit it into a meaningful video or DVD.

Whereas many projects in this book rely solely on shooting new video, this project may require spending more time gathering existing materials because, in essence, those materials can become your "shoot." It's best to assemble as many of the materials as you can—photos, audios, VHS tapes, and digital video—before you begin to edit. This often means making a trip to the basement, the attic, and the computer, and you may need to email other family members for their photos and/or videos, too.

A family memory movie can take many forms. You might want to use only scanned images to make a slideshow movie, using Movie Maker's quick and easy AutoMovie feature. Or you might want to tape interviews with family members, especially older ones. Family reunions also provide a great opportunity to shoot footage of family history, so you should consider whether this might be a part of your project. The following sections provide a few simple tips for getting your project on track.

Don't Put Yourself on a Tight Time Schedule

You don't want to stress yourself out over this project and make it not the fun process it can be. If you're using dozens or hundreds of photos in your family memory movie, you should expect that editing will take longer than if you were editing video alone.

On the other hand, it's good to have some sort of loose deadline for yourself—such as December 1 if you're going to give copies of your family memory movie to family members at Christmas, for instance—so you will actually finish your project.

Ask Others to Help

You can make your family memory movie into a family project. You can ask family members to send you photos and/or footage and get others to help with simple things like scanning photos.

Start Simple

You can start with no video at all—making a photo slideshow with digitized pictures and music as your first project—and then get more elaborate with your family memory movies over time.

Grow Your Project Organically Over Time

While it's nice to think you can gather all your materials at once, it often takes time to get your hands on all the elements. New material is constantly being created, too, so you might want to plan to update your memory movies over time.

Think (and Act) Like an Archivist

It's important to archive and label all your files well so that if you ever need to reassemble them to make a new video or DVD, for instance, you can easily locate them in appropriate folders and Movie Maker collections.

It's a good idea to invest a little time in correctly labeling images and videos. If you share these elements with others, they will also appreciate the care you've taken to include accurate filenames. You might want to come up with a naming convention that includes information such as dates (at least by year) in filenames. It's easier to share editing tasks with a helper if your images, files, folders, and collections are well organized than if they're a jumbled mess.

Creating Photo Slideshow Memory Movies

Few things are more moving than putting together pictures taken over the course of a lifetime. Looking at all the photos together, showing the passage of time, is a powerful experience—whether you're celebrating a life that's unfolding or making a memorial video of a life well lived.

Getting Organized

The easiest way to make a family memory movie is to edit photographs together and add music. Here's how you get organized to make a photo slideshow family memory movie:

1. Get your undigitized photos onto your computer. The more choice images you have to select from, the better your photo slideshow will be. Every picture tells a story—and a series of pictures tells a bigger, better story.

2. Pull your photos out of family albums, scan them, and put them back in the albums. This can be a time-consuming process, but you can do it gradually over time. Digitizing is satisfying, almost mindless work that can be a relaxing chore on weekday night or other off-time, especially if you only do it in hour-long sessions. Pace yourself so you can enjoy the task itself and don't feel resentful about having to do this grunt work. Listening to music or the radio may make the work more enjoyable.

3. As you scan and import the images into the computer, name the images and organize them in a Movie Maker collection (if you are using Movie Maker to edit your video). You can make one collection or several separate collections, organized chronologically or around a time period or theme (for example, you can organize your photos by decade or holidays).

When you have all your images in collections, you're ready to use Movie Maker or other editing software to create a slideshow movie, as described in the following sections.

> **TIP**
>
> You can find more details on importing photos in Chapter 3. And you can find more detailed instructions on making a slideshow movie at the Microsoft website, at www.microsoft.com/ windowsxp/using/moviemaker/expert/ northrup_02december02.mspx.

A Sample Slideshow Movie: A Memorial

Figures 9.1 through 9.17 are some images from a memorial movie I helped make for a friend and her family when her father, a professor, passed away. During the last few months of his life, my friend's family recorded audio with him and took hundreds of photos of him, of family gatherings, and of visits from friends. Now that he is gone, all those memories are all the more precious.

To make this video, we scanned hundreds of old family photos, imported digital photos, recorded audio interviews, imported old film footage from the 1940s, and edited all the elements together in a series of slideshows, audio, and video. All the work paid off in the three-DVD set we made.

FIGURE 9.1
As a child.

FIGURE 9.2
His parents.

FIGURE 9.3
During the war.

FIGURE 9.4
Vintage film from postwar France.

FIGURE 9.5
The Paris years.

FIGURE 9.6
More from the Paris years.

FIGURE 9.7
With his future bride.

FIGURE 9.8
Marriage.

FIGURE 9.9
Holiday photo.

FIGURE 9.10

The professor at his desk.

FIGURE 9.11

At the same desk many years later.

FIGURE 9.12

A trip to Russia.

FIGURE 9.13

With his grandchildren.

FIGURE 9.14

With his daughter on his birthday.

FIGURE 9.16

In the garden.

FIGURE 9.15

With a friend.

FIGURE 9.17

Memorial DVD Menu.

ADDING MOTION TO PHOTOS IN YOUR SLIDESHOW MOVIES

Want to make an awesome slideshow movie that looks more like a video? While a Movie Maker slideshow movie is easy to create, it still seems a bit like, well, a slideshow. To make a cinematic slideshow, you can add motion—pans and zooms—to your photos. This adds a lot of life to your slideshow.

This is the same technique that PBS filmmaker Ken Burns's popular documentaries use to create entire programs, although his films are also interspersed with interviews. (Although filmmakers have used this technique for decades, many people now think of panning and zooming across photos as the "Ken Burns effect.") You can view video trailers of Ken Burns's programs at www.pbs.org. Or you can rent his documentaries (on topics such as baseball, jazz, and the U.S. Civil War) to see how powerfully you can use this technique.

Although Movie Maker doesn't offer this feature, you can easily add motion to your photos by using Microsoft Photo Story 3 (see Figure 9.18). You can download a copy at www.microsoft.com/windowsxp/using/digitalphotography/photostory/default.mspx.

FIGURE 9.18
Microsoft's Photo Story 3 website.

Editing Photo Slideshow Memory Movies

To edit a slideshow movie in Movie Maker, you first need to import your scanned photos on your computer and place them in a Movie Maker collection. To do so, you follow these steps:

> ### TIP
> Movie Maker's AutoMovie is great for making photo slideshows with music. In AutoMovie, you can select the Movie Video setting if you want Movie Maker to time your slides to the pace of the music, which adds a professional touch to your movie. See Chapter 3, "Editing Basics: Movie Maker and More," for more detailed information about AutoMovie.

1. In the Movie Tasks pane, in the Capture Video section, select Import Pictures and then select the photos you want to import.

2. When Movie Maker imports your photos, it automatically makes each one into a five-second video clip.

3. After you have imported all the photos you want to use, drag the photos into the order in which you want them in the Storyboard view at the bottom of your screen. You can edit the length of the clips if you want to by using the Timeline or Storyboard view.

4. If you want to add music, use Import Audio or Music under Capture Video (in the Movie Tasks pane) to add it to your collection.

5. Drag the music into the storyboard. If you want to move the music around, select the Timeline view to control the music more easily.

6. If you like, add titles, effects, and transitions.

7. Preview your movie.

8. When you have all your clips and music in the order and length you want them, save and share your movie.

Digitizing Old Movies and VHS (and Other Format) Tapes

It seems like half the battle in making family memory movies is figuring out how to import old films and VHS or other videotapes into your computer. in the following sections cover a variety of techniques that help you digitize this material so you can edit it into your movie.

Digitizing Films

Old film footage is often the most difficult material to figure out how to digitize.

Many people opt to have it digitized by a professional service. You can find a supplier online or by asking your local photo shop for recommendations.

A homemade method for importing old films is fairly simple, and the cost is free, but the quality may not be as good as you would get by sending it out to a professional service.

If you want to digitize your old films at home and you have a film projector that can project the old films (it needs to be the same format as your film), you can simply shoot the movies with a digital camcorder. You project the film onto a screen or white wall, set up your tripod, and shoot the film with your video camcorder.

You can use Photo Story 3 alone to make a video CD (that plays on a DVD player) or to import finished Photo Story movies into Movie Maker for further editing.

In addition, most of the advanced editing software programs listed in Chapter 10, "Resources for Learning," can also add motion to your photos. You can see online demos of these products for more examples of what adding motion to your video can add to your movie. You'll be surprised at how much entertainment value you get from adding motion to photos in a slideshow.

You can use the power of image searches on the Internet to add material to your family memory movies.

Don't have a photo of a place that is important in your family history? For example, is Great Aunt Bertha talking about how your family emigrated from Berlin in 1895? Searching the Internet for historical photos can turn up some wonderful and surprising finds that you can import into your family memory movie. To test this, I went to Google and searched for "Berlin 1895 photo"; up popped a French site with photos. I followed another link from that site and arrived at someone's AOL page, which provided beautiful scans of vintage postcards of old Berlin, including some from 1895.

You can use an image search at your favorite search engine to narrow the results and preview many photos onscreen. And you can save any uncopyrighted photos to your computer and import them into your Movie Maker collection. If a photo is copyrighted, you should contact the copyright owner for permission to use it.

Although you should respect copyrights on any photos you find on the Web, many old photos are not copyrighted.

You need to make sure to align the edges of the film with the frame of your camcorder shot so the outer edges of the film footage don't show in the digitized version.

Digitizing VHS (and Other Format) Tapes

There are a potentially bewildering array of methods for importing VHS and other older media formats into a PC. To keep it simple, the following sections cover importing VHS tapes into a PC by using a miniDV camcorder.

VHS is an analog video, not digital, format. In order to edit it on a computer, analog video needs to be digitized.

Using a Camcorder to Digitize Your VHS Tapes

The process of digitizing VHS footage by using a VHS player and a miniDV camcorder is fairly simple. Basically, you make a *copy* ("dub") of your VHS tape onto your miniDV camcorder, and then you import the miniDV footage as you normally would onto your computer.

If you have S-VHS or Hi8 tapes, the method is the same: You just substitute *S-VHS* or *Hi8* every time you see *VHS* in the following instructions.

> **NOTE**
>
> Some newer camcorders have a special pass-through feature that allows you to simply pass the video from your VHS player through your camcorder directly to your PC. This feature eliminates the step of recording VHS video to a miniDV tape. Read your camcorder manual to find out whether your camera has this feature.

Here's what the two-step process looks like using your miniDV camcorder:

Step 1:   VHS tape → VHS player (camcorder or VCR) or TV → MiniDV camcorder

Step 2:   MiniDV camcorder → PC

Although it may seem complicated, this is actually pretty easy to do. Here's what you do:

1. Connect your miniDV camcorder to a VHS VCR or VHS camcorder.

2. Record the VHS video onto your miniDV camcorder (using external jacks on both devices).

3. Using the appropriate cables, connect either your VHS player or TV (connected to your VHS player) to the camcorder. (If you need help identifying what kinds of jacks you have, consult your VCR and camcorder manuals.)

4. Push Play on the VHS source and at the same time push Record on your miniDV camcorder.

5. After you have the VHS material recorded onto a miniDV cassette, connect your camcorder to a computer and import the miniDV footage as you normally would.

NOTE

If you don't have a VHS player, you can buy an analog capture card for your PC to import your tapes. A few of the most popular brands are Dazzle, ATI, and Hauppauge. But it's better to borrow or rent a VHS player and use your miniDV camcorder to import your video because the results will be better quality than you get with analog video capture cards. It is also more expensive to buy an analog capture card than to borrow or rent a VHS player.

6. Edit your VHS footage, which has been digitized (by your miniDV camcorder) and is now on your PC.

Archiving VHS Footage Directly to DVD

If your *only* goal is getting your VHS footage onto DVDs—say, for archiving or viewing purposes—and you don't need or want to edit the footage, you can consider buying a VHS/DVD combo recorder. These cost about $250+ new, and you can find them for $200 or less on eBay.

If you don't want to invest the money permanently, you could still consider buying a combo recorder, converting all your old VHS footage, and then selling the combo player (on eBay?) after your project is finished, if you don't have an ongoing need for transferring VHS tapes.

A number of manufacturers, including Panasonic, RCA, GoVideo, and JVC, make VHS/DVD combo recorders.

NOTE

While the convenience of these combo players is tempting, if you want to *edit* your video, using your camcorder to import it from a VHS player is a better choice. The camcorder process will give you higher-quality video compared to importing DVD footage.

Other Methods for Digitizing VHS Tapes

Having trouble importing old tape formats into your camcorder or computer? All is not lost.

If you cannot play your old videos on a player and connect either the player or an S-VHS cable from your TV to your camcorder (and record it), as a last resort, you can play the older tapes on your TV and shoot them with your digital video camcorder. It's inelegant and results in a loss of quality, but it works.

When you shoot, you need to set up your tripod and make sure to align the edges of your camera's frame so the shot doesn't show the edges of your TV.

TIP

If there's a geek in the family who wants to check out the myriad other methods for getting VHS tapes onto your PC, or if you want more details yourself, consult the popular PapaJohn Movie Maker website, at www.eicsoftware.com/PapaJohn/MM2/MM2.html.

Getting Ready to Shoot an Oral History Movie

An oral history is someone talking about their life. It involves recording someone's memories to create a living history of a person's unique experiences. An oral history can be about a particular event, a time, or an entire lifespan. It can be an interview with grandparents or older relatives. Most essentially, an oral history is the best way to record and preserve family history.

An oral history movie begins with the right preparation, including both the technical and creative aspects of your shoot:

- ▶ On the technical front, you need to review the essential equipment to bring to your shoot, as well as think about bringing extra, helpful items.

- ▶ On the creative front, what shots would you ideally like to have in your finished movie? We'll review what shots are most important to get and a list of other shots that are "nice-to-haves."

You need to bring to your shoot your camcorder, power cord, tripod, and a clip-on microphone. Audio is very, very important in shooting family memory movies, especially oral histories. Your camcorder mike will not be able to record your interviewee's voice well enough to hear it audibly on your video.

Here is a list of essentials you should bring with you to your shoot:

- ▶ Camcorder
- ▶ Videotape
- ▶ Tripod
- ▶ Power supply
- ▶ Fully charged batteries
- ▶ Extra charged batteries
- ▶ Your camera's power cord (for recharging batteries)
- ▶ External microphone and audio extension cord

In addition, you should bring any photos, old movies, or video you want your interviewee to talk about.

Here is a list of other equipment you should consider taking with you:

- Extra batteries
- Duct tape (to cover audio extension cords or power cords)

Shooting an Oral History Movie

You should prepare for your oral history movie by writing down a list of questions ahead of time. If you already know the person you're interviewing, you can ask him or her about things you are curious about in the person's life. The following sections present lists of questions you can use to dig into the details of your interviewee's life.

Asking Questions About Birth and Childhood

You can use the following list of questions to explore the person's early life in detail:

- Where and when were you born?
- What were your parents like?
- Who were/are your siblings?
- Where did you go to school?
- What were your childhood and your education like?

Asking Questions About Adult Life

You can use the following list of questions to explore the person's adult life in detail:

- How did you meet your spouse?

- How did you get your first job? What was your big career break?
- How old were you when you had children, and what was your family life like?
- When did you move from one place to another?
- Did you take any memorable trips?
- What were your most memorable family holidays or vacations?
- What are your favorite foods?
- When did you have grandchildren?

Asking Questions About Broader Themes

If it's appropriate, you can also ask questions about your interviewee's life that address themes. What does the person want other people to remember—about a certain time, about the family, about him or her?

Tips for Conducting Your Interview

Here are some additional tips for conducting your interview.

Using Photos to Prompt the Interviewee for Specific Memories

If there are photos (or old movies or videos) you want to know more about, write down your questions about the photos and bring them with you to the interview. Having props is a great way to get people talking.

Limiting Your Interview to a Comfortable Length of Time

If your subject is a senior, you should plan to interview the person for no more than an hour (or less, especially if the person is not in good health). You can schedule additional follow-up sessions if you need more time with the person.

Providing Questions in Advance

If your interviewee wants to or would benefit from seeing the questions in advance, you can share your list of questions with him or her ahead of time. That way, the person will have time to think about what to say.

Promising to Provide a Copy of Your Edited Movie

You might offer to give your interviewee copies of the interview if he or she can would like one, so he or she can review your edited version and ask you to remove anything he or she doesn't like.

Choosing a Quiet, Comfortable Setting

In shooting an oral history, you should arrange to interview the interviewee in the quietest place you can find. A private place is best so you won't be distracted or interrupted.

It's a good idea to make pleasant conversation to put the person at ease while you're setting up.

Asking for Permission to Use a Clip-on Microphone

You should put the camera on a tripod and explain that you would like the interviewee to use a clip-on microphone so the audio will be the best it can be.

If video makes your interviewee uncomfortable or if you want to create a more intimate setting, you can record an audio-only interview with your camcorder.

Conducting a Good Interview

You should ask your questions and give your interviewee plenty of time to answer. If he or she doesn't remember something, you can come back to it at a later point during this interview or a follow-up session.

Remember that your role is to get the interviewee to talk. You don't want to interrupt the person. It's what that person says that's most important to your videotape. But if you like, you can be in the video, too.

If you allow the interviewee to tell you what's on his or her mind, you might uncover new material you never knew about the person.

Directing an Interviewee Who Needs Help

If your interviewee gives an answer that is too long or too detailed, you can ask the person to repeat it more succinctly, or, if the answer is too short, you can ask more detailed follow-up questions.

Including More People in Your Shot

Often people are more at ease if you interview two or three of them together because they overcome their natural camera-shyness if they have other people to relate to. You can also choose to be in the video with them.

TIP

For more ideas and tips about interviewing family members, see the web page "How to Interview a Relative" by Kimberly Powell, at http://genealogy.about.com/cs/oralhistory/ht/interview.htm.

Considering Making a Transcript of the Interview

You might want to transcribe the audio from your interview to edit it more easily or to share it with others. A transcript gives you a written version of everything that was said, which you could give to family members or include in print or on a CD or website.

Shooting a Family Reunion

Videos of family reunions are great to have on their own as well as in family memory movies.

To shoot a great family reunion video, you can follow the shooting tips outlined in Chapter 5, "Project 1: Creating Birthday Party and Baby Movies," and Chapter 8, "Project 4: Making School Play (and Other Live Event) Movies." You can also refer to the relevant tips in this chapter on shooting oral histories.

As part of your family reunion movie, you might want to take people away from the gathering to a quiet place for a few private on-camera interviews.

Editing Family Memory Movies

Once you've organized and digitized all your photos, old movies, VHS videotapes, and any new material you've shot, you're ready to edit your family memory movie.

Even though you may have an overwhelming wealth of sources to edit, remember that as in editing other movies, you should create sequences. You'll find that once you structure your elements into sequences, you can get the editing process in gear. As you may have learned in other project chapters in this book, the easiest way to create a video is to edit visuals to music. You can also use audio alone or a combination of music sequences and audio sequences.

Family memory movies may be more challenging to make than other videos in this book, due to the number of different sources you may need to use for them. In addition, it often takes more time to edit photos than video because photos don't last very long onscreen compared to the duration of most video shots. It's important to take your time. You should edit some chunks and take plenty of breaks. You want to make the process fun. On the other hand, you may also find yourself swept away in a deep state of concentration, spending long hours at the computer, if you get into the flow; feel free to go with that, too!

FINDING THE PERFECT MUSIC FOR YOUR FAMILY MEMORY MOVIE

Adding great music to your family memory movies will bring more personality and life to them. Finding the perfect music for your movies is easier than ever, using (legal, of course) free or low-cost music download sources on the Internet.

For family memory movies, some of the best places to find music are on CD, at FreePlay Music (www.freeplaymusic.com), and at the Apple iTunes Music Store (www.apple.com/itunes; which offers 99¢ downloads).

Here are some of the best songs to add a special touch to your family memory movie:

- ▸ "In My Life" (Johnny Cash)
- ▸ "Old Chunk of Coal" (Billy Joe Shaver or other artists)
- ▸ *"Je Ne Regrette Rien"* (Edith Piaf)
- ▸ "Circle Game" (Jim Harmon)
- ▸ "You've Got a Friend in Me" (Randy Newman)
- ▸ "It's a Wonderful Life" (various artists)
- ▸ "Solilai" (Pierre Bensusan; instrumental)

TIP

Do you want to have a family memory movie made for you? A number of services will make them for you, including me (see www.strayer. com) and my Emmy Award–winning friend Susan Davis (see www.paintboxfamily.com, which is shown in Figure 9.19).

Basic Editing Steps

When you've collected everything you need for your family memory movie, you should take time to look at your footage. You need to review your elements to see what you really want to import. It's important to select only the best material. As you work with your material, you should edit out anything doesn't work— either by trimming and tightening it up or by deleting it. Gradually, the strongest material will rise to the surface, and you can polish it to perfection.

Here's a quick review of the editing steps outlined in Chapter 3:

1. Select the best portions of your footage and organize your coverage into sections that are roughly organized as a beginning, a middle, and an end.

2. Import photos, audio, music, and video into your computer and insert them in a Movie Maker collection.

3. Select the clips you like best and place them in the order in which you think they should appear in the Timeline view or Storyboard view. Edit your shots into sequences.

4. Trim your clips.

5. Edit your clips together, using dissolves.

6. Add music.

Many services on the Web, including www. paintboxfamily.com, can create family memory movies for you.

7. Add titles, effects, and closing credits. Titles are a powerful and creative tool, and they can be especially helpful in family memory movies. (To refresh your memory, you can reread the sidebar "Using Titles to Tell a Story" in Chapter 3.)

8. Review your edited rough cut and evaluate it.

9. Review your edited fine cut and make any final changes.

10. Save, share, and enjoy your edited movie.

Summary

In this chapter you've learned how to create family memory movies, using a wealth of material, including photos, old movies, VHS videos, and new footage.

You've learned how to make photo slideshow videos, add motion to your photos, and find historical photos on the Internet that can add more life to your family memory movies.

This chapter also covers the variety of ways you can digitize old movies and VHS tapes so you can edit them on your computer and include them in your family memory movies. It also shows ways to archive VHS footage directly to DVDs.

In the shooting department, in this chapter you've gotten in-depth instructions on how to shoot oral history interviews as well as brief tips on capturing family reunions.

Having so many resources available to you should enable you to make family history and memory movies that audiences will enjoy for years to come. And don't forget: Family history is ongoing, so keep shooting!

CHAPTER 10

Resources for Learning

You've learned a lot in this book, but this is just the beginning of what you can explore in making your own digital movies. This chapter covers resources that will help you further develop your skills.

This chapter lists resources for getting better at shooting and editing on your PC, and it also provides some information about new directions in which video is moving: cell phone videos, video blogs, video contests, and more. It's a big and constantly growing pond, so find out about jumping in with some of the newest video toys and action!

The field of digital movies is exploding and, luckily for us, the ability to make videos more easily and cheaply is also coinciding with the wider availability of videos on the Internet. Making movies is part of a global transformation that is changing the way we share experiences and information in both personal and public life. People are beginning to express themselves by using videos, to deepen personal relationships as well as to inform people about significant events and experiences.

As you learn more about making digital movies, you can grow your skills by making more kinds of videos than the ones described in this book. As you get more comfortable with what you have learned, you can try your hand at making longer and more complex videos— music videos, documentaries, narrative films, and more. When you've mastered the basic skills, the world's your oyster.

First, this chapter covers in-depth resources to help you polish your movie-making skills. Then it takes a look at some of the latest video developments and shows how you can have fun with them.

> **NOTE**
>
> The highly esteemed sound and movie editor Walter Murch was the first major motion picture editor to cut a big Hollywood movie, the $80 million *Cold Mountain*, on a Macintosh (using Final Cut Pro). You can learn all about this historic turning point in digital history in the book *Behind the Seen: How Walter Murch Edited Cold Mountain*. To watch Murch online in a keynote address on the future of film and video, visit www.pqhp.com/cmp/dvxw04.

Polishing Your Skills and Upgrading Your Tools

No matter how much you learn, there's always more to discover in digital movies. Camcorders and video editing software are constantly getting easier and more powerful. The following section helps you learn how to improve your shooting skills, a topic that is often overlooked, as well as how to find more robust editing tools.

Learning How to Shoot Better

In researching this book, I thought I would find lots of other information in print and online to help you become a better cameraperson. While I found lots of information for professionals, the educational resources for learning how to shoot lag behind the information on consumer video editing. Hopefully, more information targeted to your needs will be coming soon. This book is part of the next wave.

So, besides using the resources mentioned throughout this book, one good way to learn to shoot better is to review your footage. Take out a tape you shot and study it. See how you could have shot it better. Are you panning and zooming too often? How's the lighting? Would it have been better if you had used a tripod? Where might you have shot sequences—including long, medium, and close-up shots? While this can be a humbling experience, it helps you see what to do next time you shoot.

You can also take classes on cinematography to learn more about the subject. But the simple act of looking at what you shot and evaluating it yourself is a great step to take if you want to improve your skills.

You can also study TV shows, DVDs, and movies online to see how great videos are shot.

Improving Your Movie Maker Skills

As mentioned earlier in this book, this book is a guide to helping you master just enough of Movie Maker's editing features to be able to make your first videos. As I promised, in Chapter 3, "Editing Basics: Movie Maker and More," you only had to learn just what you needed to know to make basic videos. But there's much more you can do with Movie Maker. You can find out about other Movie Maker features in these resources:

- ▶ **Books**—Many books cover *every* feature in Movie Maker. One of the best is *Digital Video with Windows XP in a Snap* by Greg Perry.

- ▶ **Websites**—Because so many people use Movie Maker, you'll find lots of websites devoted to editing with Movie Maker. In addition to the information available on Microsoft's Movie Maker website

LEARNING MORE ABOUT DOCUMENTARY FILMMAKING

Want to learn more about documentary filmmaking? The book *The Art of the Documentary: Ten Conversations with Leading Directors, Cinematographers, Editors, and Producers* by Megan Cunningham (see Figure 10.1) features interviews with many of the greats. Reading about their experiences can help you develop your own video-making skills.

FIGURE 10.1

The Art of the Documentary features interviews with Ken Burns, Errol Morris, and other leading documentary filmmakers

Featured are Ken Burns, the director of many of PBS's most popular documentaries, including *The Civil War*, *Jazz*, and *Baseball*, as well as Errol Morris. Interviews with documentary pioneers D. A. Pennebaker and Albert Maysles add a

continues

historical context to learning about the field of documentaries.

If you want to go inside the world of professionals working in this increasingly popular genre, this is the best guide to the territory. Each filmmaker reveals in-depth details of the documentary filmmaking experience, with firsthand stories about the making of many widely seen movies you may have seen in theaters, including *Gimme Shelter* and *The Fog of War*. Reading the book and watching the filmmakers' movies can teach you about making your own digital movies.

(www.microsoft.com/windowsxp/using/moviemaker/default.mspx), here are some of the most popular and helpful sites created by others:

> ▸ **PapaJohn's Windows Movie Maker—**www.eicsoftware.com/PapaJohn/MM2/MM2.html

> ▸ **Windows Movie Makers—**www.windowsmoviemakers.net

▸ **Email Newsletters—**You can subscribe to Papa John's Movie Maker newsletter. For $20, it's well worth it. You can see sample newsletters online at www.windows-moviemakers.net/PapaJohn/Index.aspx.

▸ **Microsoft's Windows Movie Maker newsgroup discussions—**Visiting discussion boards is a wonderful way to learn more about Movie Maker from other users. Microsoft's Windows Movie Maker discussion board lets you post questions and search listings for important tips and help. See www.microsoft.com/windowsxp/expertzone/newsgroups/reader.mspx?dg=microsoft.public.windowsxp.moviemaker&lang=en&cr=US.

▸ **Online video tutorials—**Online video tutorials are another great resource for learning how to use software. These two sites currently offer video-based Movie Maker (and other software) training:

> ▸ **Atomic Learning—**www.atomiclearning.com/moviemaker2

> ▸ **Lynda.com—**www.lynda.com

Upgrading Your Editing Software

Movie Maker's biggest advantage is that it's free and already comes on most PCs. But you'll find many other video editing software programs available, for both the PC and the Mac, that will enable you to take things many steps further.

What do you get for purchasing more in-depth editing tools? Power, control, and flexibility in editing—as well as DVD creation features—in one streamlined package.

TIP

To find the latest news and reviews on video editing software, check www.cnet.com and www.pcmag.com.

Many of these programs give you 10 or more audio channels, more titles and title animation choices, the ability to edit picture in picture, the ability to insert pans and zooms, superimpose digital backgrounds (with chroma key), and the ability to burn DVDs with attractive, interactive menus. Some of these programs provide video email postcard art and other visual enhancements. They also support more video formats so you can output your video to a broader array of file types. And most come with automatic movie editing features similar to AutoMovie.

These software editing tools are sophisticated but also easy enough to use at home or with a classroom, and they generally cost under $100—a small price to pay for all this functionality. Some offer 30-day free download trials so you can see how they work. Many of them are available as paid downloads, so if you decide to purchase such a product, you can get it right away.

If you're planning to burn DVDs, buying a program that enables you to do it is a must—

and if you buy one of the following programs, you'll get full-featured editing software included in the deal. Even if you're not planning to make DVDs, you can upgrade to one of these programs to make editing faster, easier, and more fun.

NOTE

Everything you've learned in Movie Maker will help you learn how to use other video editing programs more quickly than if you were just starting out. (Knowing how to use Movie Maker is not, however, required, to get started with any of these editing software packages.) When you know how to use one video editing program, it's easier to learn another program. So don't be afraid to upgrade to try a better tool; it won't be like starting from scratch.

Most of the following editing programs have helpful online demos, and several offer free trial downloads, so check them out, and you'll get a better sense for how they work and what they offer:

▸ **ROXIO's Easy Media Creator**—The most popular PC program for creating videos and DVDs, Easy Media Creator lets you use as many as 14 audio tracks in a movie. It also has a more sophisticated AutoMovie-like feature called CineMagic, which offers a variety of templates. Every year, Easy Media Creator cleans up on the awards circuit, rating at the top of the heap in digital video circles with editors at *PC Magazine* and CNET. For more information, visit www.roxio.com or www.sonic.com.

▸ **Sony's Vegas Movie Studio+DVD**—Vegas Video has been a leading editing program for years. Recently acquired by Sony, the consumer version Vegas Movie Studio+DVD is now available. You can get a 30-day free trial download at www.sonymediasoftware.com/Products/ShowProduct.asp?PID=932.

▶ **Ulead VideoStudio**—There's a reason Ulead VideoStudio earned *Learning Magazine*'s Teacher's Choice Award for the best video editing software: It's really easy to use and has a lot of great features. You can see an online demo and download a 30-day free trial at www.ulead.com/vs/runme.htm.

▶ **Adobe Premiere Elements**—For years, Adobe Premiere has been one of the leading professional editing software makers. Now Adobe's new consumer video editing software program, Adobe Premiere Elements, is available. You can see an online demo at www.adobe.com/products/premiereel/main.html.

▶ **Pinnacle Studio Plus v9**—The best-selling consumer video editing software, this full-featured package provides everything you need to make great videos. Plus, this website offers tips on shooting and editing in online demos. You can see the online demo and a get a free 30-day trial copy at www.pinnaclesys.com/howto/default_US.asp?langue_id=7.

▶ **iMovie HD**—Editing on a Mac? Apple's iMovie HD is a full-featured, easy-to-use consumer video editing software program. iMovie HD comes bundled in iLife, a suite of digital media products from Apple that ships free on new Macintoshes. It's also the first consumer video editing software program for editing high-definition movies. For more information, see www.apple.com/ilife/imovie.

The Latest Video Trends

According to Kevin Maney of *USA Today*, "Everything that has happened to words and photos the past 10 years will happen to video in the next 10" ("Tech show expects video to flourish on Net the way words have," *USA Today* January 9, 2005).

More and more video content is moving onto PDAs, cell phones, personal video players (PVPs), and the Web. While making videos can be a personal art form, it can also be used for broader social uses for play and for work. The following sections explore mobile media, video blogs, and cinema contests—all entertaining new media anyone can have fun with!

Mobile Media

As you'll see, video isn't just for TV or DVD players anymore. PDAs, cell phones, and PVPs let you take your video with you. Here are just a few of the many examples of emerging platforms for playing with video on the go.

PDAs: Pocket PC

Want to share your video wherever you are? Save your video to Pocket PC. One of Movie Maker's sharing options lets you select Save for Pocket PC and gives you a variety of file types to choose from. This is a great way to show off short home videos.

You can access this option in the Save Movie Wizard in Movie Maker or get more details online, in the article "Optimizing Windows Movie Maker Video for Pocket PC Devices," at www.microsoft.com/windowsxp/using/moviemaker/expert/bridgman_02november18.mspx (see Figure 10.2).

Cell Phone Video

Many new cell phones feature video cameras that let you take small, low-resolution videos that you can import into a PC for editing. If you have a cell phone that is capable of shooting video, you can learn how to import this video into your computer. Consult your cell phone manual or contact your cell phone provider for details. (The quality is bound to improve over the next few years!)

Figure 10.3 shows an inspiring and pioneering example of cell phone video creativity. You can watch the first music video shot on a cell phone—*Haber Get Down*—at http://ghettron.textamerica.com/?r=455355. Although this video was shot on a cell phone, it was edited on a Macintosh. Some of the very latest video cell phones will soon let you edit video on the cell phone.

FIGURE 10.2

The Microsoft website features information on using Movie Maker to create videos for Pocket PC.

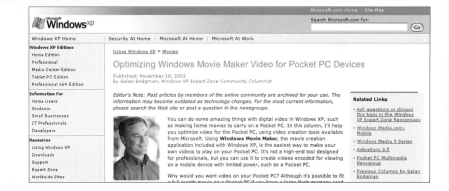

FIGURE 10.3

Haber Get Down, the first music video shot on a Nokia 3650 cell phone.

Here are some resources to help you stay up-to-date on the latest mobile media:

▶ **Engadget**—Engadget is one of the best places on the Internet to stay current on all kinds of new digital devices, and it is one of the few sites that tracks PVP developments. Explore http://portablevideo.engadget.com to find out about new PVP devices.

▶ **David Pogue/*New York Times*—**At www.davidpogue.com you have free access to all of Pogue's articles from *The New York Times* as well as his free email stories and his daily blog. Pogue is one of the funniest and most irreverent technology writers, and he tells readers the real story about the marvels of technology. Written in a personal, approachable style, his site praises the best and mercilessly skewers the worst of new consumer computer gadgets and software. You can sign up for his email newsletter to get his latest missives delivered to your email inbox.

▶ **Walter Mossberg/*Wall Street Journal*—**For a 90-day free access to Mossberg's columns, visit http://ptech.wsj.com. Perhaps the most respected of all the mainstream technology press, Mossberg and his assistant personally test the latest technology gadgets and tell you the pros and cons of new devices. This site features a complete archive of all of Mossberg's columns. He also appears in weekly videos about his latest personal technology column on www.cnbc.com.

▶ **CNET and *PC Magazine*—**These two also provide extensive coverage of personal technology. You can visit them online at www.cnet.com and www.pcmag.com, respectively.

PVPs

PVPs, which have just started coming onto the market in the past few years, allow you to carry VHS or better quality videos with you, depending on the size and cost of the PVP. (However, they don't allow you to shoot video.)

Many PVPs on the market today haven't taken off because they're big, expensive, and use heavy hard drives to store videos.

But one player is both cheap ($99) and small—ZVUE from HandHeld Entertainment (see Figure 10.4). You can put short or long videos on it; the length and quality of your video files depends on the size of the SD/MMC card you put into your ZVUE. ZVUE is currently available online at www.walmart.com and in selected stores. For more information about ZVUE, go to www.zvue.com.

FIGURE 10.4

The ZVUE PVP has won rave reviews from many magazines and websites for its low cost, video quality, and ease of use.

Video Blogging

While video blogs may seem ultra-new-fangled, you'll see that they can be a fun, easy, and inexpensive way to make and share videos. They can be a tool for self-expression and keeping in touch with family and friends, as well as a new source of news. In the wake of the 2004 tsunami, video posted by ordinary people became an important way to share news about the disaster.

Blog stands for web log, and a blog is usually a form of personal writing posted online. This definition is rapidly expanding to include video. Video blogging (vlogging) generally involves posting of personal videos to an Internet site, where they can be seen by others.

Often, vlogs are personal narratives or diaries—or even diatribes. But they can be used for many different purposes. Vlogs can be used for education and business as well as personal newscasts.

While most vloggers use webcams and camcorders to record their videos, many video cell phone manufacturers are rapidly starting to promote vlogging as a way of selling new phones.

Blogs of all kinds, including vlogs, can become more powerful when users subscribe to blog feeds by using RSS (a free simple subscription software) and get updates about new postings. And many sites are becoming vlog aggregators, where you can find lots of vlogs to explore.

THE BEST VIDEO (AND VLOGGING) SOFTWARE: VLOG IT!

By far the most exciting editing software introduction I have seen in years is Vlog It! from Serious Magic (see Figure 10.5). It's great for anyone who wants to make professional-looking videos, using either a webcam or camcorder, without having to learn how to edit at all.

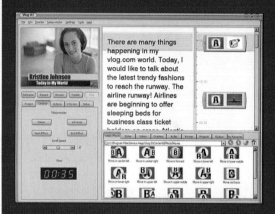

FIGURE 10.5
Using Vlog It! is an easy, inexpensive way to make videos.

In fact, the only thing wrong with Vlog It! is its name, and that's because many people are likely to think you have to be interested in vlogging to use it. In fact, Vlog It! is a great video creation tool that anyone can use to make personal videos more quickly and easily than anything I have ever seen. It brings ease of use to new heights.

Vlog It! (and its cousin Visual Communicator) lets you create your own personal newscast right in front of your computer. You type in what you want to say and drag and drop photos and videos to the places in your text

continues

where you want them to appear. You turn on your video camera and read your script, just like newscasters read a teleprompter, and Vlog It! automatically inserts your photos and videos when you get to that the appropriate point in your transcript.

The program also lets you add slick digital titles (and digital backdrops, if you shoot against the right background) to your videos, and it features an impressive selection of motion graphics (designed by professional broadcast animators from major motion networks).

Vlog It! is sure to make anyone the star of a very professional-looking video, even if you have never made a video in your life. The product is amazing, and the price is even more mind blowing: just $99.95 for what may be the only video software you need.

See the sidebar "Popular Vlogs on the Internet," later in this chapter, for some great examples of the more popular vlogs.

Here are some of the best resources on the Internet for learning more about vlogs:

▸ **Wikipedia's vlog listing**—The free Internet encyclopedia Wikipedia offers a good introductory overview of vlogging and links to many more resources online. It is updated constantly by users, so it provides links to the most current information. Visit http://en.wikipedia.org/wiki/Vlog.

▸ **Yahoo! vlogging group**—Want to see and learn more about vlogs? You can subscribe to vlogs or hear what vloggers are up to by visiting the very active Yahoo! group on vlogging, at http://groups.yahoo.com/group/videoblogging.

▸ **Freevlog**—For the best overview on how to set up a vlog, check out Freevlog's website (see Figure 10.6), where you can find video tutorials that show how to save Movie Maker videos to use in blogs, get free blogging software and video hosting, and enable RSS subscriptions to your vlog. Details are available at www.freevlog.org.

▸ **Cell phone vlogging**—Nokia's Lifeblog is one of a number of new video cell phone features to help cell phone video camera users share and edit their videos. You can learn more at www.nokia.com/nokia/0,,71739,00.html.

Vlog Hosting

A group of nonprofit sites on the Internet allow you to host your video files for free:

FIGURE 10.6

Freevlog.com provides a one-stop website for all you need to know to create your own video blog.

- **Our Media**—Our Media is an Internet website that provides free hosting for video files. Get the latest information at www.ourmedia.org.

- **Internet Archive**—Internet Archive (see www.archive.org) is an organization dedicated to helping preserve Internet files. Visit the tutorial "Making a Vlog in Windows XP" to see a video with step-by-step instructions on how to make a vlog, The Internet Archive is actively supporting the vlogging community (including free hosting) and provides thousands of (non-vlog) movies to watch in its Moving Images channel.

- **Creative Commons Publisher**—You can upload your video to www.archive.org by using free software available online at the Creative Commons website, www.creativecommons.org/tools/ccpublisher.

POPULAR VLOGS ON THE INTERNET

Vlogs are like the "real" reality TV, covering the Internet, politics, technology, and fun stuff. The following are some of the best examples on the Internet.

- Rocketboom—More than 25,000 visitors per day come to see Amanda Congdon, an actress, do a flip, and see funny daily Internet culture newscast on her site, www.rocketboom.com (see Figure 10.7).

- Steve Garfield's Blog—This vlog is created by Boston-based video maker Steve Garfield (see Figure 10.8) and can be seen online at www.stevegarfield.com. Steve's blog features interviews, escapades, and videos on many different subjects, but one staple series is "The Carol and Steve Show," a takeoff on the 1950s sitcom a la 2005. Watch "Episode 28: Part 2" to see how great vlogging is for sharing cooking tips, as Steve and Carol show off using a new clean grill, flip burgers, and share their recipe for Boston baked beans (see Figure 10.9). Garfield is a professional video editor, so the quality of his web videos is better than that at the average vlog site. His vlog videos have even been picked up for distribution in the "real world" of cable television.

- The First Politician's Video Blog—With help from Steve Garfield, Boston City Councilor John Tobin is the first politician to launch a vlog. You can see it online at www.votejohn-tobin.com/blog/Videos (see Figure 10.10).

- Ryanne's Video Blog—Ryanne Hodson is a New York video editor who's a popular vlogger with the classic type of vlog—an online video diary. Check out http://ryanedit.blogspot.com (see Figure 10.11).

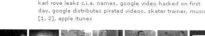

FIGURE 10.7

Amanda Congdon does a daily *Saturday-Night-Live*-like newscast on Rocketboom.com.

FIGURE 10.8

Steve Garfield's vlog offers high-quality videos.

FIGURE 10.9

The Carol & Steve Show is a regular feature on Steve Garfield's professional-looking vlog.

FIGURE 10.10

John Tobin is the first politician in America to use a vlog.

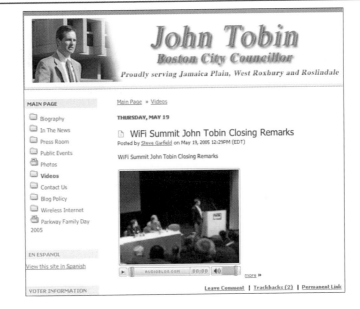

FIGURE 10.11

New York editor Ryanne Hudson's vlog is an online video diary.

Video As a Sport

While blogging represents a video trend that emphasizes quick-and-dirty first-person videos, other video makers have taken their creative efforts in a different direction.

Cinemasports is one of the most fun and creative new ways to play with video. Cinemasports, which calls itself the Iron Chef of filmmaking, sponsors competitions in which filmmakers make miniDV videos—including scripting, shooting, and editing—in just 10 hours!

As in a scavenger hunt, teams are given a list of ingredients that must be in their films. Screening of finished films, which each must be at least 3.5 minutes in length, begins 10 hours later the same day!

Cinemasports has become an international event and is well on its way to being a regular part of some film festivals. Check the website www.cinemasports.com to see completed videos, award winners, a blog of participants, and a calendar of upcoming events so you can find out how and where to participate in the next Cinemasports event yourself (see Figure 10.12).

FIGURE 10.12

Cinemasports.com, which bills itself as the Iron Chef of filmmaking, runs competitions for making videos from start to finish in one day.

Summary

In this chapter, you've learned tips, tools, and trends that will help you take your digital movies to the next level. This chapter covers the importance of periodically reviewing your footage to see how you can improve and provides a comprehensive list of the most popular and powerful editing programs, many of which you can also use to create DVDs.

In addition, you've gotten a chance to explore emerging trends in digital video on mobile devices and taken a look at the wonderful world of vlogging, which is changing the meaning of personal media to a realm beyond shared digital photos. You've seen how vlogging is also emerging as a public medium, affecting network television's coverage and the way politicians communicate with their constituents.

By now, you have discovered that there are many ways you can jump into the exciting world of making your own digital movies. See how far you can go, using all that you've learned in this book and the most valuable treasure of all—your own creativity. Enjoy your video adventures!

Index

What's on the CD-ROM

The companion CD-ROM contains a trial version of Adobe's Premiere Elements and a trial version of Pixélan's SpiceFX packs for Movie Maker 2.

Windows Installation Instructions

1. Insert the disc into your CD-ROM drive.

2. From the Windows desktop, double-click the My Computer icon.

3. Double-click the icon representing your CD-ROM drive.

4. Double-click on **start.exe**. Follow the on-screen prompts to access the CD-ROM information.

> **NOTE**
>
> If you have the AutoPlay feature enabled, **start.exe** will be launched automatically whenever you insert the disc into your CD-ROM drive. Windows may hide the file extension of **start.exe** so you may see **start** instead of **start.exe**.